SUTTON POCKET HISTORIES

THE
BOER WAR

FRED R. VAN HARTESVELDT

SUTTON PUBLISHING

First published in 2000 by
Sutton Publishing Limited · Phoenix Mill
Thrupp · Stroud · Gloucestershire · GL5 2BU

British Library Cataloguing in Publication Data
A catalogue record for this book is available from the British
Library.

ISBN 0-7509-2248-6

Cover photograph: Afrikaners equipped with modern bolt-action
rifles during the Second Boer War, *c.* 1900. (Hulton Getty)

 ALAN SUTTON™ and SUTTON™ are the
trade marks of Sutton Publishing Limited

Typeset in 11/14 pt New Baskerville.
Typesetting and origination by
Sutton Publishing Limited.
Printed in Great Britain by
Bath Press, Bath, Avon.

Contents

Acknowledgements

Writing is a solitary effort, never done alone. A number of people gave help so willingly to this book that it would be wrong not to thank them formally. Jerry Brown, Obioma M. Iheduru and B. Keith Murphy, my colleagues at Fort Valley State University, read the manuscript and made valuable suggestions. My friend Kenneth Saladin at Georgia College and State University did likewise. Another friend, A. Franklin Brayman, in Birmingham, Alabama, contributed from his amazing knowledge of military hardware and tactics. My wife, Mary Ann, was not only patient while I worked on the manuscript, but also helped with the dreary work of proofreading and reference finding. Each of these people did more than anyone could expect. Any errors or infelicities of phrase that remain are clearly my own fault.

List of Dates

15 December. Battle of Colenso.

18 December. Lord Roberts appointed to replace Buller as commander in chief.

1900 **24 January**. Battle of Spion Kop.

11 February. Roberts begins his campaign.

15 February. Kimberley relieved.

18 February. Battle of Paardeberg.

28 February. Ladysmith relieved.

13 March. Bloemfontein occupied by the British.

17 May. Mafeking relieved.

28 May. Annexation of the Orange Free State.

31 May. Johannesburg occupied by the British.

5 June. Pretoria occupied by the British.

15 July. Steyn and De Wet leave Brandwater Basin.

3 September. Annexation of the South African Republic.

19 October. Paul Kruger leaves South Africa.

29 November. Lord Kitchener replaces Lord Roberts as commander in chief.

1901 **28 February**. Middleburg peace talks.

1902 **11 April**. Battle of Roodewal.

15–18 May. Initial discussions at Vereeniging.

31 May. Surrender signed.

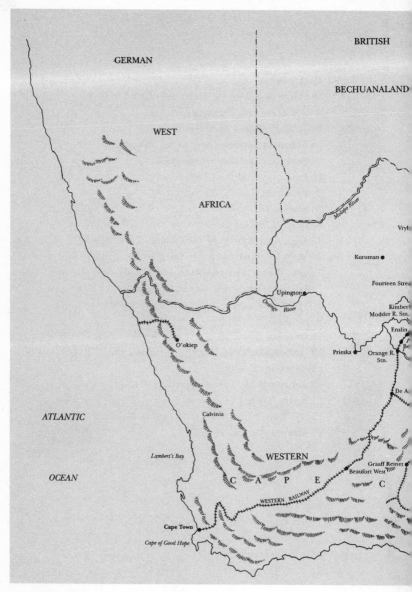

General map of South Africa during the Boer War.

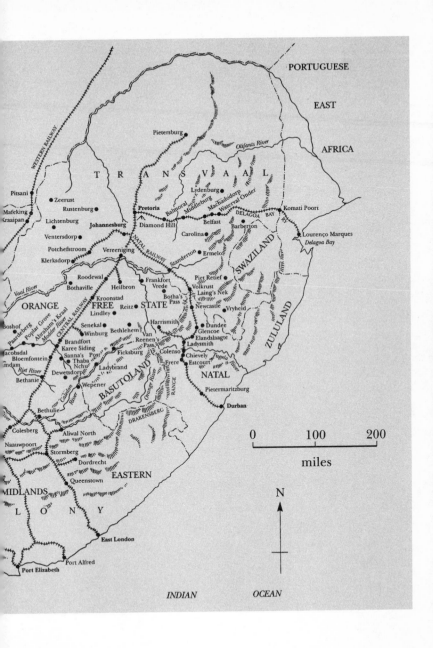

ONE

Origins

The original European settlers at the southern tip of Africa were Dutchmen, who arrived in the seventeenth century to establish a port of call for ships doubling the Cape of Good Hope. Although the Dutch had no intentions of establishing an extended settlement, some of them stayed and were joined by a significant number of Huguenots fleeing the persecutions of Louis XIV in France. These Frenchmen brought knowledge of Mediterranean farming techniques, which were appropriate for the climate, and the colony prospered. Their descendants became known as Boers from the Dutch word for farmer. Over the next two hundred years they developed a language, Afrikaans, and a sense of national identity that led them at the end of the nineteenth century to militarily challenge the British Empire.

The British came to the southern tip of Africa in the late eighteenth century due to the Napoleonic

Wars. The Netherlands became an extension of Napoleon's empire, and the British, unwilling to allow a naval base as strategically located as the Cape to fall into the hands of an enemy, seized the colony. At the end of the conflict, Britain, the greatest naval power in the world, needed strategic bases for its fleets and decided to pay the Dutch £6,000,000 and keep South Africa.

The change of ownership did not initially make much difference, but by the early 1830s there were problems. A mix of changing economic conditions and humanitarian sentiments led to the abolition of slavery in the British Empire in 1833. The Boers did not care for interference in what they regarded as their freedoms and were fearful that in the long term their political dominance would be undermined by the growth of democracy. A number of them, including the young Paul Kruger, who would eventually lead them into war in 1899, moved north in what is often called the Great Trek, and established what were ultimately to become two small republics: the South African Republic (commonly called the Transvaal) and the Orange Free State.

The indigenous peoples of the region, especially the Zulu, fought bitterly for their land, but in a triumph of will and firepower, the Boers finally – but sometimes narrowly – won control. Their key victory came at Blood River on 16 December 1838. For the moment, the British authorities saw no reason to play Pharaoh to the Boers' Israelites, for imperialism was not regarded particularly favourably at that time. However, in 1842–3 Britain took Natal, blocking the Boers's access to the sea. In the Sand River Convention of 1852 London recognized the independence of the South African Republic. Two years later the British withdrew from land north of the Orange River which became the Orange Free State. British interest did linger, and they later took islands in Delagoa Bay, ensuring that the Transvaal remained landlocked.

In 1867 diamonds were discovered along the Orange River, which created an economic boom. The city of Kimberley was founded in 1871 and soon became the centre of an enormously lucrative industry. In that same year London annexed Griqualand West – the diamond region – brushing aside the vigorous protests of the inhabitants of the Orange Free State. The Boers were developing a deep distrust of the British. They were particularly concerned about the possibility of a British-controlled federation, including the Orange Free State, in South Africa. The first steps seemed to be granting self-government to the Cape Colony and settling the Orange Free State's claims over

Griqualand West by a payment of £90,000. In 1877 the British annexed the virtually bankrupt Transvaal to the impotent outrage of the Boers (Kruger even visited London to seek redress), and over the next few years extended their control to more and more of Southern Africa through a continuation of conquest and agreements made with native rulers.

The British had gone too far. In 1880 the Transvaal proclaimed its independence. The relatively few British military forces in the area were commanded by Sir George Pomeroy Colley, whose reputation was quite good. Unfortunately, he suffered a tactical defeat at Laing's Nek. He seems, then, to have become determined to restore his own and the Army's reputation by winning a major victory. The Liberal government, led by Gladstone, was less enthusiastic. The Liberals were uncomfortable with the idea of forced imperialism and eager to avoid spending money. Colley was told to negotiate and sent a peace proposal, but set a forty-eight-hour deadline. The message had not even reached Kruger, who headed the provisional government, when the time expired.

Feeling free to recommence operations, Colley took a force up Majuba Hill (actually Amajuba, the hill of doves) on the night of 26 February 1881. He seems to have thought that seizing the high ground

4

to dominate the Boers's position meant victory. He carried neither guns nor rockets with which to bombard that position, planned no attack by the rest of his force and once on top declared his men to be too tired to entrench. Ian Hamilton, one of Colley's officers, would later deny the last. The Boers, once they got over the consternation of rising on Sunday morning to find British soldiers looking down on them, soon realized that the angle of ascent meant they could climb the hill in relative security from small arms fire. Climb they did. The fight that followed was one of the more inglorious for the British. Highlanders, supposedly the cream of the Army, fled in disorder and Colley was killed, some say trying to surrender, though others insist he went down revolver in hand trying to rally his men. The result may be judged by the fact that Majuba Day became a national holiday for the Boers. Although actual losses were not devastating and reinforcements were arriving, Gladstone had had more than enough. He sought peace. On 5 April 1881 the Treaty of Pretoria was signed. It gave the South African Republic independence subject to a vague assertion of British suzerainty, whatever that might mean.

Following this there were various developments that in retrospect were clear steps towards the much larger war that began in 1899. Both British colonial and Transvaal territory expanded. In 1880 Cecil Rhodes, who personified British imperialism, organized the De Beers Mining Company to exploit South African diamond mining, and in 1883 Paul Kruger, the symbol of Boer independence, was first elected President of the South African Republic. In 1884 the Convention of London settled some territorial issues between the South African Republic and Great Britain, but although the Boer government was prohibited from signing treaties without London's approval, there was no mention of suzerainty. Whether this omission was, as the Boers interpreted, a withdrawing of British control, or as the British thought, the non-reiteration of established fact, has never been clarified. London, pressed by the German desire to find a place in the imperial sun, continued to expand and consolidate in South Africa. The Boers were not forgotten, for St Lucia Bay was annexed to Natal, once again ensuring that Pretoria did not possess a port.

A dramatic change came in 1886 when massive gold deposits were discovered on the Witwatersrand in the Transvaal. A gold rush brought many prospectors (Uitlanders, or outsiders, to the Boers) to the Rand region. Rhodes, having moved to stabilize his control of diamonds, expanded into the gold industry. London, whether the motive was gold or imperialism, continued to seek domination of the area. Zululand was annexed in 1887 to block yet again Transvaal's access to the sea, and talk of a federation – at least economic if not political – was renewed. Kruger would have none of the latter, and was increasingly concerned that his country was being surrounded by British territory – Cape Colony to the south and south-west, Natal and Zululand to the east, and British Bechuanaland to the north-west. Furthermore, his nation was being inundated with immigrants.

At this point, much of the drama began to centre around Cecil Rhodes. He was gaining control over Matabeleland (later to become part of Rhodesia), north and west of the Transvaal, through his South Africa Company (chartered in 1889). He was dreaming of a South African Federation. In 1890 he became Prime Minister of Cape Colony and began to forge an alliance with the moderate nationalists of the Afrikander Bond (a nationalist political party in the Cape Colony that was willing to make accommodations with the British). He made concessions about the required use English and began to promote racist legislation. Although far from a democracy, Cape Colony did have a limited black franchise. Rhodes knew that unless he made the Cape conform with the rest of the region there was little hope of federation.

Rhodes also thought that moderates, who might be inclined to compromise about British power, would win control of the Transvaal government, but to his dismay in 1893 Kruger won a third five-year term. Hoping for the best, Rhodes sought to arrange a customs union. Although the Orange Free State was agreeable, Kruger rejected the idea out of hand. The Transvaal president was concerned about annexations. The British had strengthened their hold over the east coast by first taking Pondoland, tying Cape Colony to Natal, and then Tongoland, blocking Kruger's last hope of controlling direct access to the sea. London had acted on Rhodes's urging, and it was more his aggression than London's that Kruger needed to fear. Kruger did have the opening of the Delagoa Bay Railway line to cheer him, which meant rail access to the sea through Portuguese territory. He tried to shift trade patterns away from the Cape and to the new line by imposing prohibitive rates on shipments between Johannesburg and the Vaal River. When shippers used ox wagons to cover that short distance, Kruger retaliated by closing the drifts (fords) of the river. An ultimatum from London brought this economic confrontation to a close and unfortunately gave Rhodes and others a false sense that Kruger lacked the courage of his convictions.

During his years of empire building, patience had
been the hallmark of Rhodes's success. Now he was
in a hurry. Geological surveys of Matabeleland had
established that it had no gold field like the Rand.
Rhodes's Chartered Company was threatened with
ruin if this information was made public, unless he
gained control of the Rand first. Furthermore, his
health, never good, gave him reason to think he no
longer had time to be patient. He began developing
a plan to take advantage of Uitlander discontent.
The Uitlanders had come to make money, and often
had. Nonetheless, they did have some grievances. To
protect against a block vote, the Transvaal
government had promulgated a fourteen-year
residency requirement for suffrage. It also applied
surtaxes on foreigners and created economic
monopolies that forced miners to pay well above
market prices for some goods. The dynamite
monopoly was particularly hated.

Rhodes got London to transfer a strip of land
along the Transvaal border to his Chartered
Company, supposedly for railway development. In
fact, it was to be a base from which a paramilitary
incursion into the Transvaal was to be launched. The
precipitating factor was to be an Uitlander revolt in
Johannesburg. When the rebellion, with the aid of
the raiders, was successful, the British High

Commissioner in Cape Colony, Sir Hercules Robinson, would arrive and mediate a settlement that left the British in control – a federation in practice if not name. The raid was to be led by Dr Leander Starr Jameson, a long-time employee and friend of Cecil Rhodes. Little went right. Uitlander support, apparently never as strong as the planners thought, dwindled as it became clear that the intention was to establish British rule. Their idea had been to take over themselves. Joseph Chamberlain, Colonial Secretary, favoured the idea of federation and certainly knew the general outlines of Rhodes's plan. He insisted, however, that the raid culminate in raising the Union Jack. He was not willing to do more than appear to respond to appeals to save the Uitlanders, who, despite their mixed origins, could be presented as abused subjects of the Queen. He made clear to Rhodes that nothing was to happen until the Johannesburg revolt began. The revolt seemed increasingly unlikely. Jameson requested instructions, but Rhodes's order to stand down did not reach him in time. Rhodes may have wanted to say he sent the order but not actually stop the raid. So Jameson led his force into the Transvaal.

To say that the results of the Jameson Raid were embarrassing would be an understatement. The

Uitlander revolt was a non event, though the putative leaders were arrested. The raiders were quickly captured without even any significant fighting. Although he tried to blame Jameson for acting on his own, Rhodes had to resign as Cape Prime Minister and lost a great deal of prestige. He avoided the loss of his company's charter by making clear to Chamberlain that he had and would publish telegrams implicating the Colonial Secretary if such action were taken. Chamberlain denied knowledge, and was later exonerated by a Parliamentary Select Committee that clearly had many interests beyond establishing the truth. To Kruger, the raid was a godsend. It proved the British threat was real, not only to his own people but also to the Orange Free State, which had previously been far more inclined to compromise. The two states concluded a defensive alliance. It was also an obvious excuse to purchase arms – though remarkably untouched personally by the allure of gold, Kruger understood how it might be used in pursuit of national defence. Kaiser Wilhelm II sent a telegram of congratulations on a successful defence against foreign aggression. This, along with other expressions of foreign support for Kruger, turned potential English shame at an assault on a relatively helpless target into jingoistic outrage. It also gave the Boers the idea, although this turned out to be false, that foreign aid would be available if they had to confront Britain again.

Although it has been argued that the raid lit the fuse that fired the explosion of war in 1899, there were some opportunities to dampen that fuse in the intervening three years. Unfortunately, sweet reason was not the hallmark of the personalities involved. Kruger, who reputedly read nothing but the Bible, drew upon his religious fundamentalism as a source of nationalist fervour. He believed himself one of God's people, and possession of the Transvaal divinely ordained. His British opponent was the new British High Commissioner, Sir Alfred Milner, urbane, Oxford educated, highly intelligent and imbued with a vision of British imperialism. They were not the two men most likely to be chosen by an impartial mediator seeking compromise. In addition to his imperial goals, Milner was concerned about the rights of blacks, though not in favour of immediate full equality. If the Uitlanders represented the possibility of an English – as opposed to Afrikaans – speaking white (voting) majority to Kruger, blacks, the overwhelming numerical majority, could completely dominate elections.

Milner arrived in the late summer of 1897 with instructions to seek a peaceful accommodation with the Transvaal. There were certainly Afrikaners who favoured compromise, but the re-election of Kruger in February 1898 suggested that such progressive elements were not influential. The election provoked further agitation by the Uitlanders. In the next few months Milner became increasingly convinced that only a policy of confrontation – war if it came to that – would give Britain the control he deemed necessary in Southern Africa. In London the government was concerned about other issues and was not inclined to belligerence. Milner's natural ally, Chamberlain, no doubt remembering the last time imperial dreams and Uitlander grievances drew him into an active polity in South Africa, insisted on negotiations. The frustrated Milner returned home in the winter of 1898 hoping to gain support through personal appeal. He achieved little change in policy, and to his outrage Sir William Butler, military commander in Cape Colony and in charge while he was away, rejected a petition for help on the part of the Uitlanders. Milner charged Butler, who certainly favoured compromise, with undermining his policy and being pro-Boer, and lobbied against him until the general was recalled.

When he returned to Cape Town, Milner was happy to accept and transmit to London a second Uitlander petition, containing more than

20,000 signatures. Hoping for a compromise, President Marthinus Steyn of the Free State proposed a summit conference between Kruger and Milner. The dubious Milner rejected any participation by moderate Cape Afrikaner politicians and went to Bloemfontein for the conference at the end of May 1899. Some say it typified the atmosphere of the conference that Milner refused to shake Kruger's hand. Milner partisans, however, have argued that he may not have noticed Kruger's gesture, or that he may have felt a handshake, before the formal opening, would violate protocol.

The negotiations at Bloemfontein may be simplified. Milner demanded full suffrage for Uitlanders after five years's residency. Kruger offered seven with some restrictions. Milner refused and on 5 June broke off the talks unilaterally, just before receiving a message from Chamberlain urging further discussion. It was not, however, the end. In July the Transvaal passed legislation granting suffrage after seven years's residency, and London proposed a joint investigation into how this might work out. Kruger then suggested five-year residency if Britain formally dropped its claim to suzerainty. Partly at Milner's urging, this was rejected and Kruger refused to continue. Kruger was now convinced that the British would have the Transvaal one way or another, while they were asserting that he sought to eliminate British influence entirely in favour of an Afrikaner confederation.

Both sides had begun military preparations. Kruger waited until the spring – October in South Africa – when the veld grass was high enough to sustain his soldiers's horses, and sent an ultimatum demanding that reinforcements be recalled and that troops be pulled back from his borders. Not surprisingly the British rejected it. Two days later, 11 October, the Orange Free State, more through honour than conviction, joined its ally. On 12 October 1899 the invasion of British territory began.

TWO

The First Months

When the war began the two sides seemed hopelessly mismatched. The largest empire in the world, with a small, professional military, against two small republics with almost entirely part-time, volunteer armies. This disparity was not quite as extreme as it seemed. The British Army had slightly over 100,000 men under arms, with a reserve of about three-quarters of that number and had to have garrisons scattered across much of the world. Furthermore, to get line units up to strength for deployment overseas it was necessary to pull men out of the reserves. Cheese-paring governments had not kept the military adequately supplied for war in the late nineteenth century, and after the war began there were soon shortages of guns, ammunition, harnesses, wagons, uniforms, in fact of almost everything the Army needed. In 1899 the government was in the hands of the Conservative (or Unionist) Party with Lord Salisbury as Prime Minister. Despite the warnings of

Milner and Chamberlain, it had remained optimistic that the problems in South Africa would be peacefully settled. The Cabinet finally agreed to send reinforcements, mostly from India, only a few weeks before the declaration of war, and few had arrived by the time the fighting started. British forces in South Africa in October 1899 numbered only about 20,000.

The Boer military was much less formally organized. Each of the two republics had a professional artillery service and had purchased modern guns mostly from Krupp in Germany and Creusot in France. Although fewer in number, these guns had a better range than the standard British field piece and the British were forced to employ naval guns to match them. The rest of the Boer forces were organized by commandos. These were small units ranging from a few hundred to a few thousand men. Commandos were associated with regions or towns and all adult men, or burghers, were obligated to join if the call came, but individuals were not required to serve with their local commando and sometimes joined another. Commandos elected their own officers – a commandant and, depending on numbers, some veld-cornets and corporals. Decisions were made by *krygsraads*, or war councils, with the men voting on what to do. Individuals might even choose to stand aside as they might grant themselves leave. Discipline was tightened during the war, particularly under strong commanders such as Christiaan de Wet and Koos De la Rey, but keeping the burghers on a battlefield, especially after a hard fight, was always a problem. Fortunately, the Boers had a tradition of fighting against the natives and a frontier type of spirit. The majority of them were tough, determined fighters who, often blessed with good leadership, did not fall prey to what would appear to be a hopeless lack of discipline.

The Boers had some other advantages. Impelled particularly by Paul Kruger, they had already armed. Their governments were ready to supply soldiers with modern bolt-action Mauser rifles. These used smokeless powder that helped conceal the user, and were clip loaded, holding five rounds. The Lee-Metford used by the British was similar, but its ten-round magazine had to be loaded bullet by bullet. The frontier life in South Africa meant that most residents grew up hunting, and thus developed some skill with firearms. They were also horsemen. Every soldier came to his commando with his own horse, a horse that was accustomed to the climate and to the tough, wiry veld grass. The British lost at least 350,000 animals largely because they failed to familiarize the horses with local conditions before making heavy demands on them. The fact that every man was mounted gave the Boers a mobility that to a significant degree defined the tactics of the war. The British were accustomed to combined infantry and cavalry forces, with greater emphasis on the former. In a war fought in an area roughly the size of France, with forces quite small by the standards of the twentieth century, mobility was a distinct advantage.

When the fighting started most of the British troops were in the area of Ladysmith in Natal, under the command of the recently arrived Sir George White. The British commander was under some pressure. Boer forces numbered about 40,000 and might invade Natal with the port at Durban as their target. They might also strike into the Cape Colony, a possibility that Milner feared and urged White to block. Such an attack, especially if successful, might result in the rebellion of the Cape Dutch, citizens of the colony who regarded themselves as Afrikaners and supported a Boer victory. This threatened loss of British control in the entire region. In addition, Natal political authorities told White that any defeat that left the appearance of weakness could result in revolt by local native tribes. Strategists, then and later, argued that the best course was to fall back and defend Natal from behind the Tugela River.

Such a withdrawal, however, meant giving up Ladysmith and defending a very long line with a force made up mostly of infantry. Instead, White decided to fortify Ladysmith, where his supplies were stockpiled, believing that the Boers would not be able to bypass such a strong position.

Boer strategy seems somewhat unclear. They wanted to eliminate British forces on their borders and stop the advance of reinforcements, but these were really more tactical than strategic goals. Their 1881 victory at Majuba was strategic because its suddenness resulted in London's decision to negotiate, but repeating such a victory depended on an unlikely renewal of the British irresolution of 1881. A more likely strategy was to invade Natal and the Cape Colony and deny the British use of the ports and railroads. This would force British troops to land in other colonies or on the beach and march overland just to get to the battlefields. At the beginning, when they had a numerical advantage of perhaps two to one and the possibility of support from the Cape Dutch, such an effort had a real chance of success. Unfortunately for their cause, a caution that dogged Boer decision-making throughout the first year of the war already prevailed.

Before White's arrival, his second in command, Major-General Sir William Penn-Symons, led British forces out of Ladysmith to the town of Dundee. Penn-Symons was an aggressive officer with an arrogance born of fighting foes armed with primitive weapons. His idea was to put the boot to the Boers and bring the contest to a quick end. At the Battle of Talana, 20 October 1899, the British sustained 464 casualties and 250 captured. Penn-Symons himself received a mortal stomach wound when he stepped in front of the line to gauge the situation. The Boers, led by Piet Joubert and Lucas Meyer, lost 132 killed. Nonetheless, the British held the field and accounted it an expensive victory. Penn-Symons's second in command, Brigadier-General James Yule, however, was forced to abandon the wounded, including Penn-Symons, and make a very difficult 45-mile forced march back to Ladysmith, covered in part by a successful attack against the Boers at Elandslaagte on 21 October. Elandslaagte demonstrated the abilities of Sir John French as cavalry commander and Ian Hamilton with the infantry, but the force was quickly pulled back to Ladysmith.

White was not yet convinced that offensive action could not help protect Ladysmith. At the end of October he sent forces to attack Long Hill, which proved to be unoccupied, and the troops soon came under fire from nearby Pepworth Hill. The commander, Colonel G.G. Grimwood, lost control of the situation and White pulled the force back. White had also sent troops under Lieutenant-Colonel Frank Carleton to Nicholson's Nek as a protection for his left flank. En route the mules carrying ammunition, artillery, and other supplies stampeded and returned home. Carleton, who had never before commanded in combat, however, went ahead. The Boers attacked and the British suffered 143 casualties and had about 1,000 men taken prisoner on what came to be known as 'Mournful Monday', 30 October 1899. White returned to fortifying Ladysmith, where he had perhaps 13,000 soldiers and about 8,000 other people. The siege was underway.

Meanwhile, on the western side of the Transvaal, Colonel R.S.S. Baden-Powell had been sent to raise some local forces in Rhodesia and defend the border. In case of war he was to raid the Transvaal in hopes of occupying Boer troops while the British waited for reinforcements. He was not welcomed at the Cape. Soldiers resented being superceded and Milner feared that the plan would make it more difficult to portray the Boers as the aggressors in the war he was hoping was soon to begin. Baden-Powell found it hard to get supplies and was ultimately ordered to conduct his business in mufti and forbidden to recruit in Natal and the Cape Colony, though he did so secretly. Although he never got any modern artillery, his supply situation was much improved when one of his staff officers, Lord Edward Cecil, a younger son of the Prime Minister, offered a personal guarantee for purchases of £500,000.

Two regiments were finally raised. One was stationed in Rhodesia under Lieutenant-Colonel Herbert Plummer, and the other in Bechuanaland near the borders of the Cape Colony and the Transvaal. The quality of the recruits was, however, poor. They were mostly drawn from men who lacked other prospects and few had prior knowledge of horsemanship or firearms. Their numbers were relatively small – less than a thousand per regiment when the war began – and the likelihood of training them well enough to make significant raids into enemy territory approached zero. So like White, Baden-Powell began to consider defending a fortified position, which the Boers would have to invest. Mafeking, a railway junction and administrative centre where his supplies were beginning to pile up, was the obvious choice, but because it was just over the border into Cape Colony, he had to accommodate Milner's refusal to outrage the colonial government with military preparation. Baden-Powell surveyed the defences and got his people into place in the guise of supply dump guards. When the war opened, he was ready except for artillery – he had only relatively short-range muzzle loaders. During the siege an eighteenth-century brass cannon buried muzzle down as a marker was exhumed and refurbished. It was, of course, a smooth-bore muzzle loader, but its range exceeded anything else in Mafeking. With it Baden-Powell was able to ensure Boer artillery was kept at a distance.

Baden-Powell also began, even before the siege, a campaign of trickery to help keep his foes at bay. There was a large quantity of dynamite in Mafeking. It was intended for industrial use and not adaptable for military purposes. It was loaded on a train and sent out of town, where the carriage was abandoned. Boer fire detonated the contents, and although apparently none of the enemy was actually hurt, Piet Cronjé, who commanded the investing force, and his men were left with no doubt that the defenders had explosives. Baden-Powell then announced that he was going to mine the approaches to the town, but that to protect people and their livestock the mine fields would be clearly marked. He had his engineers make hundreds of boxes, fill them with sand and bury them in the 'mine fields'. He and a few officers then rigged charges of explosives to a few of these 'mines' and had a test. As he had confidently expected, word quickly reached the Boers. Although fake mines seem like the stuff of adventure magazines and films, the Boers clearly respected the 'mine fields', and Baden-Powell settled down to stand one of the most famous sieges in history.

When he discovered that the Boers did not attack on Sundays, Baden-Powell organized and participated in sports, theatricals and other entertainments on those days. On one occasion he ordered a sortie against Boer artillery and marked the return path with red lights in his own lines. He then disrupted the enemy's routine by putting up red lights from time to time so that further attacks were expected. When asked to surrender to avoid further bloodshed, he declined because there had not yet been any. After a bombardment, he posted a casualty list that began 'Killed: One Hen'. He has been accused of shameless self-promotion for exaggerating the importance of Mafeking, the number of besiegers and his own nonchalant behaviour, but he provided the British people with a symbol of resistance and determination that helped buoy their spirits during times when all other news from South Africa seemed to herald disaster. He became one of very few British heroes of the Boer War, and even if his fame was based more on public relations than military achievement, it seems nonetheless to have been important.

The final siege was further south. The city of Kimberley was the centre of the enormous diamond mining industry in South Africa and, like Mafeking, was on the Western Railway. Its importance from the military standpoint was limited, but it certainly symbolized the great wealth of the region and was the headquarters of De Beers, Cecil Rhodes's firm. Furthermore, Rhodes himself, having resumed some political role since the embarrassment of Jameson's Raid, had rushed from his Cape Town home seeking a role in the war. He was a target not welcomed by defenders, but he ended up in Kimberley, where he was at times an enormous help and at others a thorn in the side of the military commander, Lieutenant-Colonel Robert Kekewich.

Deference was not Rhodes's hallmark, and so while Kekewich mounted guard from a watch-tower and tried to parry the Boers with a much inferior force, Rhodes either found useful work to do or fretted and made trouble. In the beginning, the tycoon helped organize and equip – even with rifles – the defending force. The amount and variety of supplies that came out of company warehouses was astounding. George Labram, an American engineer in the company's employ, was put to work making bullets and then a muzzle-loading cannon that allowed the defenders to reply to Boer siege guns that out-ranged all the Army artillery in Kimberley. As the Creusot guns shelling the city were called

'Long-Toms', it was perhaps inevitable that Labram's creation was christened 'Long-Cecil'. In an ironic twist, Labram was killed by a shell during the siege.

Rhodes had been the centre of attention for so long, however, that he found not getting what he wanted difficult. Helping to defend Kimberley grew tedious, though in the material sense he never stopped doing so. When Rhodes wanted to get news and conduct business and found that military communications were not freely available to civilians, he arranged his own. Native runners came and went through the Boer lines, and if the charges were high (as was the cost of being caught), Rhodes could afford them. He was soon in regular communication with Cape Town and even London. He could get messages to the military authorities sometimes more expeditiously than Kekewich. His mercurial nature, sense of self-importance and serious underestimation of the Boer military led him to expect and then demand that Kimberley be promptly relieved. To Kekewich's discomfort, Rhodes exaggerated the difficulty the defenders faced – actually, thanks to the bounty of Rhodes's company, the people of Kimberley were the least deprived of any of the besieged communities. The soldier and tycoon were on increasingly bad terms and eventually hardly spoke. Finally, Rhodes announced that if he were not guaranteed a date for relief he would call a meeting of the townspeople to discuss options. Kekewich and his superiors feared this meant surrender, and the colonel was told to prevent the meeting and arrest Rhodes if necessary. However, calm prevailed and the siege continued. But Kekewich was placed in the awkward position of trying to deal with a man with Rhodes's political influence who was supplying large amounts of materiel to his forces and whom the people of the city were likely to follow in preference to military authority. To his superiors, Kekewich seemed unable to control his command and unfortunately his reputation never recovered.

The opening campaigns of the war gave the British little to be pleased about. Their forces in South Africa were almost entirely trapped in sieges, and the Boers seemed free to strike the Cape Colony and Natal if they chose. The British were also concerned about the loyalty of the Cape Dutch, and no one knew the likelihood of native unrest. There were some hopeful signs, however. Reinforcements were en route and more were ordered. The widely respected General Sir Redvers Buller was to be sent to South Africa to command. His superiors, the government and the people expected him to achieve a decisive victory. Oddly, he was not so sure he was the right man for the job.

THREE

Buller's Campaign

At sea Sir Redvers Buller missed getting news of the initial fighting in South Africa. Travellers on a passing steamer held up a sign announcing three unnamed victories and the death of Penn-Symons. Buller's travelling companions worried that the war would be over before they even arrived, and with only this hint of intelligence the new commander landed in Cape Town on 31 October 1899 – the day after 'Mournful Monday' which had seen the defeats at Nicholson's Nek and Pepworth Hill. His ignorance, while not surprising to a Victorian, was in retrospect a harbinger of British difficulties throughout the war. The Army put little emphasis on staff training or work and although Buller expressed satisfaction with the officers assigned to him, doing so may have reflected acquiescence in Hobson's choice. In addition, the respected General Archibald Hunter, appointed his chief of staff, had been detained in Ladysmith by Sir George White, who blithely said he was needed there.

Furthermore, there was no premium on intelligence-gathering in the Victorian Army, which spent only a fraction of what other great powers of the day did on the effort. The result was that Buller was not only ignorant of the immediate situation but also of Transvaal and Free State military capacities. The maps he was provided with were typically inaccurate, out of date or drawn on an inappropriate scale for planning military campaigns. The problem was made worse in many cases because those in tactical command had neither information about the enemy nor about the ground over which they were to fight. Moreover, many lacked awareness of the importance of such information and did not have the skill to obtain it, even if they had wanted it. Thus ignorance became one of, if not the most, significant factor in causing British problems in the campaigns to come.

Buller's plan involved using the Central Railway as a supply line and driving into the Orange Free State and then the South African Republic, taking their capitals (Bloemfontein and Pretoria), and accepting the expected surrender in triumph. It was reasonable. He expected to have the needed mass because an Army corps of some 47,000 men was en route. The troops already in South Africa could continue to defend and the corps could be employed for the offensive. Using the railway as the line of advance would compensate for the relative paucity of mounted troops and supply units. Making the capitals his objectives followed the traditional pattern of European war – in the most recent, the Franco-Prussian War, the Germans had driven on Paris. In reality, traditional objectives had little value in the Boer War, but expecting Buller to realize this in the beginning was ridiculous.

Upon arrival, however, Buller found the situation changed. Most of the British troops in South Africa were besieged in Ladysmith, with, of course, smaller forces at Kimberley and Mafeking. There was a real threat of Boer invasion into Natal and/or Cape Colony with the potential of creating rebellion and closing sea ports vital to British logistics. The civil authorities continued to express concern about the potential for native uprisings – the good account that the Zulu, Basuto and others had given of themselves in recent times was not forgotten. The besieged cities did not represent very vital strategic points militarily, but the loss of Kimberley would mean that the enemy held the centre of the lucrative diamond mining industry (by 1890 £39,000,000 worth had been extracted) and Cecil Rhodes might be captured or killed. The loss of any of the towns would be symbolically damaging to the prestige of the Empire and encourage the Boers as well as other potential trouble makers. Buller was forced to confront a problem that has discomforted many generals before and since – the political implications of military decisions.

Buller changed his plans and divided his forces. His decision has been praised as the best possible choice given the combination of political and military issues, and damned as denying the British adequate mass to win decisively at any point. Like most decisions of this nature, the judgement tends to be based on the outcome, which in this case was not very good. A case can be made that the result was only partially Buller's fault and that had the men he assigned to lead been more effective he would now be the hero of the Boer War rather than the goat.

The new plan called for Lord Methuen to push north along the Western Railway with his division, about 12,000 men, and relieve Kimberley. Lieutenant-General William Gatacre with a smaller composite force was to move into the central part of Cape Colony toward the railway junction of Stormberg. Buller, himself, would accompany the largest force to relieve Ladysmith in Natal. This contingent, composed of sixteen infantry battalions, eight batteries and two cavalry regiments, was technically under the command of Major-General C.F. Clery, but the presence of the supreme commander meant that Buller would, in effect, lead the force. The week of 10 to 16 December was destined to be remembered as 'Black Week' because each part of Buller's force suffered setbacks. However, these were not all as disastrous as popularly believed at the time.

The first battle was at Stormberg. Gatacre was determined to attack, but from the outset made errors. Inept handling of communications resulted in a unit of 400 men not being told to report for the attack, but despite their unexplained failure to appear, the operation went ahead as if they were in place. The route of advance in the initial plan was changed at the last minute, and the new orders did not reach all units. Medical and other support units following the original route were destined to stumble into the enemy until warned by newspaper correspondents, who, following the same route and thinking they were lost because they could not find the combat troops, had returned. Gatacre, 'Backacher' to Tommy Atkins, was a man of notable vitality. No amount of physical stress seemed to wear him down, and he tended to forget that not everyone was his equal. The new route was longer than the original, and he made the men march with fixed bayonets so their rifles were awkward to carry and thus more tiring. The one officer who knew the path was inadvertently left behind, and local guides led the troops in a roundabout way to the point of attack. The men, who had been up all night, were tired and hungry before the fighting even started. The assault was then diverted against a low but steep rocky hill held by a small force of Boers. This hill could have been bypassed and the main objective taken relatively easily. Instead, the combination of the ground and accurate defensive fire resulted in the attackers recoiling in confusion. Gatacre, having lost control of the situation, decided to retreat. Communications then failed him again and some 600 men were left behind and ultimately taken prisoner.

It was not all Gatacre's fault, but it was embarrassing. His main mistake was to assume that the units in his composite force, despite never having worked together before, could handle a complex and changing plan without confusion. Nonetheless, by almost any objective standard, the skirmish at Stormberg was only a tactical reverse. Gatacre held his position and could protect the rail junctions of Naaupwpoort and De Aar to his west, though like all British forces at this point in the war, he was painfully short of mounted troops. In most circumstances Stormberg would soon have been forgotten.

While Gatacre was moving toward Stormberg, Methuen, as planned, followed the Western Railway nearly to Kimberley. He won three bloody tactical victories: Belmont, Graspan and the Modder River. There was nothing subtle in his tactics. When the Boers made a stand, he ordered a frontal assault, for, in his own words '. . . I intend to put the fear of God into these people . . .'. The fighting at the Modder River was really a draw. Koos De la Rey introduced a new defensive idea. He convinced the Boers to entrench in front of the river rather than on the high ground behind. This misled British artillery, which ineffectively shelled the hills. It also allowed more effective use of small arms, for rounds fired had a flat trajectory and swept the ground in front of the trenches. Firing down from the hills, however, meant that when a bullet missed its original target it was more likely to bury itself in the ground than to hit another. Smokeless powder allowed the Boers to fire from cover without revealing their positions. Recognizing this combination of factors was a remarkable feat for an amateur soldier. It was equally impressive that De la Rey could convince the burghers to try his new tactics. Typically, burghers did not like hand-to-hand fighting and wanted to be able to reach their horses for flight before the disciplined Tommies got close enough to launch a bayonet charge. Taking position in front of the river was not conducive to getting away, should this become necessary. De la Rey won the argument, however, and after a day of serious combat, the Boers held their ground. Methuen was only able to claim victory when he awoke the next morning to find that his enemy had withdrawn during the night.

Across the Modder, Methuen was only a few miles from Kimberley, and the hills at Magersfontein were the last place that the enemy might make a stand. While Methuen pressed doggedly along the railway towards them, the Boers prepared a defence similar to that at the Modder. The commander, Piet Cronjé, initially refused, but fortunately De la Rey arrived in time and with the support of President Steyn got the new style defences in place. They expected a frontal assault, and the British general, who had only nine hundred mounted troops and lacked mobility, did not disappoint. His plan was a night approach followed by a dawn attack. The front ranks of the attack force were to be Highlanders commanded by the popular rising star of the Army, Major-General A.J. 'Andy' Wauchope. Although he seems to have had some reservations about the plan (though he raised none with Methuen), Wauchope set off in the early hours of 11 December. Methuen had no proper maps to give him and compasses were inaccurate because of ironstone in the area. Wauchope, however, found his way, and was only a little behind schedule at first light. He kept his unit in tight formation to prevent straggling and the inevitable slowing that moving into extended order meant. Just as he was about to spread his men out, they ran into a thick belt of thorn bushes and he decided to clear the obstacle before giving the order. It was a fateful choice, for the Boer defensive positions were several hundred yards closer than he thought. The Highlanders cleared the bushes, but before they could spread into extended order, their ranks were swept by a fusillade of Mauser fire. Wauchope was one of the first hit, and he was followed by most of the officers, who, though they had learned not to make targets of themselves by wearing clothing different from other soldiers, had to stand to see what the situation was.

The Highlanders were in a bad spot, but not defeated. They fell prone and tried to defend themselves. During the day that followed they were attacked by ants whose large hills provided much of the available cover, and their legs below their kilts and above their stockings were blistered by the sun. Other units in the attacking brigade did manage to extend and make a fight of it. Unfortunately, Methuen thought of no tactic other than continuing to push straight forward, though he withheld a significant part of his force from the battle, and a day of hard fighting followed. After some nine hours, a Boer counter-attack on the Highlander position forced an order for one unit to fall back. Word spread among the tired troops and a general disorderly withdrawal began. It would be too strong to call it a rout, but the Boers were left in possession of the field. Methuen held his position for the night, hoping in vain that morning would find the Boers gone, as it had at the Modder River. He then withdrew to the Modder, to the enormous frustration of Cecil Rhodes in Kimberley. The British had suffered a second defeat in two days. With almost a thousand casualties, perhaps four times as many as the Boers, this was more than a tactical setback. It was, however, less than crushing. Methuen's force was still in the field and able to fight. There was reason to reconsider tactics, but not to panic.

For the third part of the offensive, Buller's force in Natal, about 18,000 men, was to move westward along the Natal Railway to Ladysmith. Once that city was relieved, British forces were to concentrate on an invasion of the Free State and the Transvaal. As he advanced, Buller knew he would have to cross the Tugela River, a natural barrier that he expected to be defended. The railway he was following crossed near the village of Colenso, behind which there was a range of hills. When he had a look at the position, Buller thought it was too difficult and decided on a flanking march. Then word came of Stormberg and

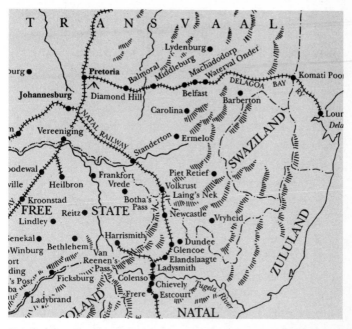

Detail of the general map showing the area of the campaign in Natal.

Magersfontein, and the general, commonly described as a bulldog, apparently had a crisis of confidence. He was again confounded by the political elements of war, and became convinced that a quick and decisive victory was vital. To get it, Buller resolved to make a frontal assault at Colenso, the position he had thought impregnable just a few days before.

The defenders at Colenso had a new commander, Louis Botha. A young man, Botha had begun the war as only a veld-cornet, but his gift for war had quickly become apparent and in the loose, informal system of the Boers he rose quickly. He had opposed allowing the siege at Ladysmith to prevent an offensive into Natal, but his aggressiveness had been checked by the elderly and cautious Piet Joubert, who agreed to no more than a small raid and withdrew that at the first setback. At the end of November, Joubert fell from his horse and went home to recuperate. At his recommendation, Botha was accepted as the new commander.

Had it been conceived by a professional soldier, Botha's defensive scheme for Colenso would have surely been regarded as masterful. Coming from an amateur in his first large unit command, it was truly remarkable. It was not without risks, for it assumed a straightforward thrust from the British, and had Buller made his originally planned flank attack and moved quickly Botha might well have seen his line rolled up. Having only about 4,500 men – the informality of the Boer military and the fact that burghers could grant themselves leave meant that even the officer in charge often did not know his exact troop strength – prevented Botha from manning an extended line in force. He read Buller perfectly, however, and had his strength in just the right place.

Botha's tactical plan was equally good. The orthodox move would have been to contest the river crossing. He did not. Although he destroyed the railway span, he left a foot bridge in place. He wanted the British to cross and then be trapped in a killing ground between his positions and the river. He placed his men in camouflaged trenches or behind natural cover below the hills, expecting British artillery to shell the high ground. He then gave orders that no burgher was to fire until he gave the signal. That the plan did not work perfectly was due more to the frictions of war than the abilities of his opponents.

Buller's plan was simple. He was not fooled by the open bridge, and sought a crossing slightly upstream where his very poor maps indicated there was a drift a little west of a large loop in the river. A brigade under Major-General Arthur Fitzroy Hart was to find this drift and force a crossing while a second brigade under Major-General Henry Hildyard was to drive directly at the village of Colenso. Both brigades would have field artillery support and the remaining two brigades would be in reserve. The longer range naval guns were also to provide support from a rise further in the rear. It was not a bad plan, though it did not provide any goal beyond forcing a river crossing. Botha had one problem and Buller a golden opportunity. There was a low mountain called

Hlangwane to the east of Colenso on the British side of the river. It overlooked Boer lines and a force on top could dominate them. Buller virtually ignored it. His mounted troops under Lord Dundonald were instructed to protect the flank on that side, the British right, and to move up the Hlangwane if possible. But it was a small force and taking the high ground was not presented as a major objective. Botha recognized the danger, but had trouble convincing his burghers to occupy it. With the river behind, the contingent on the hill would have nowhere to go if the fight turned against them. Only when telegrams from President Paul Kruger and General Joubert confirmed Botha's view of Hlangwane's importance were lots cast and the losers, a few hundred, agreed to garrison the position.

On 15 December the British attacked. Their noisy and elaborate preparations warned the Boers to be ready. British artillery fire was ineffective against their trenches and often fell on the unmanned hills. Little went right for the British that morning. On the left, Hart's brigade was misled by its guides. Instead of finding the promised drift, it was led into the deep but narrow bend in the river, which was under fire from three sides. Hart, whose concept of tactics seems to have begun and ended with a frontal attack in close order, responded by pushing more men into the loop. After the initial losses, however, the situation was not as bad as it seemed. Once they lay down and with support, Hart's units could have held their position for some time and kept the defenders in their area in place. Buller, however, called it 'a devil of a mess' and ordered General Neville Lyttleton to extract the men from the loop. Then he learned of even more alarming news.

In the attack on Colenso itself, Colonel Charles Long, in command of the supporting field artillery, had pushed his guns within 1,000 yards of Boer lines. He had gained notable success with such aggressive tactics before, but had not been fighting troops armed with modern rifles. When his twelve guns unlimbered and began to fire on Boer positions, Botha's trap was sprung prematurely. Many casualties were averted, but Long's gunners were quickly under heavy fire. In the finest tradition of the British Army, they worked their guns and by some accounts were suppressing Boer fire when they began to run out of ammunition. Long himself had taken a bullet through the liver (he would later say that the organ had been sluggish until 'the Boers tickled it up'). Seeing little cause to endure fire they could not return, the gunners retired to a nearby donga (shallow valley) to await resupply. Meanwhile, messengers sent for ammunition told Buller the artillery was in hopeless circumstances. He hurried to the scene and saw only the abandoned guns. While observing he was hit by a spent shell fragment and badly bruised, but he did not mention the injury to those around him. His will collapsed, and he ordered a withdrawal.

Disengagement was not, however, really necessary. Buller had two brigades in reserve, which might have been used to make a flanking move. Dundonald had dismounted his cavalry and gotten a foothold on Hlangwane, but when he asked for infantry support to finish taking it, Major-General Geoffrey Barton, in command of a reserve brigade, refused to act without Buller's direct order. The commander did not even know of this situation. The attack on Colenso, though stalled, might have been pressed. Long's ox-drawn naval guns had fallen behind but eventually got into position to provide supporting fire. Although Buller has been praised for being willing to withdraw and save his men, he did so before he was really defeated. Nonetheless, 145 men were dead and more than 1,200 wounded or missing.

Buller made two final and unfortunate decisions at Colenso. First, driven by the nineteenth-century sense of shame at the loss of guns, he made an attempt to save Long's. At his call volunteers came forward and two attempts were made. At the price of human and animal casualties, including Lieutenant Freddy Roberts, son of Lord Roberts, a rival of Buller's in the Army, two guns were removed. Then, as further attempts seemed futile, Buller's loss of spirit deepened and he abandoned them completely, although they might have been covered by rifle fire and probably recovered after dark. The Boers removed them later, capturing a few gunners who had not received word of the withdrawal, and virtually doubled their artillery. Buller's second decision was a message by heliograph to White in Ladysmith informing the city commander that help would be some time in coming and suggesting that he consider firing away his remaining ammunition and surrendering. Although Buller later claimed that his intention had been to make it possible for White to surrender honourably if the situation came to warrant it, the language did not make that interpretation seem valid. Once the message became public, Buller's reputation never recovered. He paid a high price for initial but not decisive defeat and even more so for a message sent in a moment of despair. The first instalment was his replacement by Field Marshall Frederick Roberts, First Baron of Khandahar.

FOUR

Roberts's Campaign

Colenso was the third defeat of 'Black Week'. In London confidence in Buller waned so much that it was decided to give overall command in South Africa to Lord Roberts, who had offered himself for the post. Roberts was told of his appointment and the death of his only son at Colenso on the same day. Popularly known as 'Bobs', Roberts was one of Britain's best-known soldiers, but elderly. Therefore, General Herbert Horatio Kitchener, Lord Kitchener of Khartoum and Aspall, was appointed chief of staff, but really acted as a second in command. Kitchener was reputedly cold, ruthless and ambitious. He was the sort of commander, unlike Buller and Roberts, who was willing for his men to pay any price for victory. His service in South Africa did not change that reputation.

Oddly, Buller remained as commander of the Natal Field Force. This has been interpreted as meaning that either Roberts made an effort to avoid even the appearance of vengeance for the death of his son, or that Roberts simply did not have a more suitable candidate available for the position. The situation was further complicated by the fact that Roberts, in the tradition of deferring to the man on the scene, made suggestions to Buller but did not issue orders. Thus Roberts's campaign began as an extension of Buller's.

Although Roberts advised that he simply stand on the defensive, Buller was determined to make another bid to relieve Ladysmith. Perhaps he hoped to regain some fragment of his lost reputation, or perhaps, as he said, he had begun to see the key to unlocking the situation. If so, it took more than one turn to rotate the tumblers. The arrival of the 5th Division under Sir Charles Warren meant that his force numbered 30,000, even larger than before Colenso. The lost guns were also more than replaced. There was a problem, however. Warren, who had been successful in fighting the Zulu in the past, was thought to be something of an expert in African war and was given a dormant commission. In other words, he was to take overall command if Buller were incapacitated. Buller seems to have resented him.

Buller's plan was very similar to what he had originally intended to do. He would move to his left and cross the Tugela at Trichardt's Drift. He put Warren in charge of the operation, though he remained close at hand. The plan had the potential to force Botha to defend a longer line than he had men to garrison effectively. For that potential to become reality, however, implementation had to be quick enough to prevent the Boers from shifting their concentration. Warren believed that thorough preparation was the key to victory, and he moved slowly. The first step came on 17 January when Dundonald's cavalry crossed the river on the left of the British position. Dundonald, showing his usual initiative, flanked the Boer position and pushed on to Acton Homes Farms, about 10 miles from Tabanyama Ridge, the right end of the Boer defensive line. He was in position to move virtually unopposed into Ladysmith. When he called for support, he was reprimanded for exceeding his orders and told to withdraw. The cavalry was only to cover the British flank and protect baggage. Dundonald had overstepped his orders. If he deserved a dressing down for that, however, the advantage he had gained should have been exploited, not foolishly thrown away. The only justification for not sending support was the British shortage of mounted troops and there seems to have been enough for such a move.

Infantry attacks began on 18 and 19 January 1900, but made only limited progress. Buller, increasingly impatient but unwilling to assert control himself, pressed Warren to get on with it. Warren finally suggested taking a hill called Spion Kop which dominated the position. Buller agreed, although neither seems to have really thought through the strategy very thoroughly. The battle that followed was an embarrassment for the generals.

Before dawn on 24 January Warren sent forces up Spion Kop. In a harbinger of command problems, he put General John Coke in command, but because Coke had not fully recovered from a broken leg, Major-General E.R.P. Woodgate actually led the column. Typically for this stage of the war, there was little information about the ground and local guides proved incompetent. Lieutenant-Colonel Alex Thorneycroft, who commanded Thorneycroft's Mounted Infantry, a unit raised in South Africa, had spent some time looking at the hill through a telescope. This limited amount of intelligence work made him the expert on the scene. He took the lead, and by repeatedly stopping the column, moving ahead and then calling it forward managed to find a way up. The British were virtually at the top before being challenged, and a bayonet charge cleared away the Boer picquet. The next step was to entrench and prepare to hold. Unfortunately, sandbags prepared for the expedition had been forgotten and some tools had been abandoned as too heavy. The light entrenching tools the men had did not penetrate rock found about 18 in down, and they were left to pile up what stones and other material they found to make a very low wall. They had no artillery, for a mountain battery planned for the attack had inexplicably not been brought from the base camp. Nor had rockets, available in the British arsenal. Worse than all of this was the fact that without accurate maps (a balloon that could have provided observations of the top of the mountain had not been used) and in a heavy fog, the British had not reached the crest of Spion Kop. They were entrenched on a secondary crest that allowed them a field of fire only about 100 yds deep. The position was also enfiladed. To their right Aloe Knoll, about 300 yds away, looked directly down their trench. Conical Hill to the front and Green Hill to the left also provided the enemy with positions that the very limited British defensive arrangements did little to block. In addition, Boer artillery was well positioned and accurate. The British counterpart was neither, and the one time it actually helped the men on the hill – by bombarding Aloe Knoll – General Warren ordered a change of target because he believed his men held the entire summit.

The burghers initially panicked when they realized the British were above them, but Botha rallied them. With his intuitive sense of military principles, Botha quickly realized that the British position on Spion Kop was poorly placed and that he was not being attacked elsewhere. Therefore, he could concentrate his limited forces against Spion Kop. The Boers seized Aloe Knoll and initiated artillery and small arms fire from other sights. They also climbed to the crest, where British units had been pushed forward to but had not yet prepared defences. The result was bitter fighting at close quarters, sometimes hand to hand. The hero on the British side was Thorneycroft, who despite a badly twisted ankle, rallied his troops again and again. On one occasion he stopped a surrender. Some 200 Lancashire Fusiliers had raised a white flag, but Thorneycroft stepped forward to order the burghers and their prisoners back to their lines. He then restored the British line with reinforcements from the Middlesex Regiment. All along the line the British held, but valour was undone by inept communications and command indecisiveness.

Woodgate had been mortally wounded and his second in command had taken charge. When word reached Warren, he ordered Coke up the hill to take over, but his bad leg slowed him down. Once there, he set up headquarters on the reverse slope and was rarely directly involved in the fray. Meanwhile, Buller, who actually had a better position than Warren, even some visual oversight of the battlefield, had sent a message to Warren expressing concern about the situation and urging that 'a real fighting man' be put in charge. He suggested Thorneycroft. Accordingly, Warren sent a message to Thorneycroft, promoting him and giving him command, but he neglected to inform Coke. Therefore, Coke and Thorneycroft each thought he had overall command. If that were not sufficient confusion, the fighting made communication along the British line limited at best. The senior officer at the end away from Thorneycroft, who had assumed command at Woodgate's death, still thought he was in charge. Thus, for much of the day three officers each thought he had command. The result was continuing disorder. A message from Thorneycroft requesting reinforcements, water and artillery support was intercepted by Coke, who, not knowing the situation, added his own suggestion that artillery was not needed. Some reinforcements came up but water remained in short supply throughout the day.

Winston Churchill, wearing his war corres-pondent's hat, went up the hill and was appalled at the situation. He hurried down and tried to report the problems to Warren. The general, whose information was that things were not so bad, dismissed him and when Churchill persisted, ordered his arrest. For once aristocratic prejudice proved useful. Though not in line to inherit the title, as a member of the family of the Dukes of Marlborough Churchill was not only above arrest, but was also allowed to go back up the hill to tell Thorneycroft that reinforcements, artillery and food and water were being sent. It was too late. Exhausted and feeling abandoned by his superiors, Thorneycroft had decided to withdraw. He would not rescind the order when he heard from Churchill or when challenged by other officers. Despite some lingering dispute about seniority – Thorneycroft had started the day as a lieutenant-colonel – no one took a determined stand against the decision. Spion Kop was evacuated.

The great irony is that the Boers evacuated too. Unaware of how badly the British had been battered and having suffered seriously themselves, they ignored the urging of Botha and left Spion Kop. In the very early hours of the morning two burghers returned to the battlefield to look for wounded comrades and, to their amazement, they soon realized the enemy was gone. They reported this and Botha was then able to get men back to the top of the hill. Had British officers listened to Churchill or others who insisted that the evacuation be stopped and/or that Spion Kop be re-occupied, the battle would now be termed an expensive British victory. In fact, Buller retreated back across the Tugela.

Redvers Buller, now sometimes called 'Sir Reverse', was not finished. Just two weeks later he made a third attempt to reach Ladysmith. Forces under General Neville Lyttleton were thrust across the river at Vaal Krantz and took their initial objectives. When resistance stiffened, Buller queried Roberts about the cost in casualties and whether Ladysmith was worth the price. Roberts urged him to push on regardless, but issued no actual orders. Instead of throwing his reserves forward and making a fight of it, Buller once again fell back across the river, becoming to some 'the ferryman of the Tugela'. Despite such disparagement, Buller remained popular with his men. He was well known for not eating before they were fed and for not risking them unnecessarily. Despite the defeats, morale was high and, finally, a fourth attempt succeeded. Buller used his full force in a series of staggered assaults that overwhelmed the Boer ability to defend, and the Battle of Pieter's Hill cleared the way to Ladysmith. Although the Boers retreated in confusion, Buller occupied himself with a triumphal entry into the city rather than continuing to advance. His limited number of mounted troops was unlikely to corner the Boers, but he could have kept them off balance and demoralized. He was formally welcomed in Ladysmith on 1 March, the besieged garrison being near the end of its endurance. A typhoid epidemic had raged for weeks, and rations had been reduced until emaciation and lassitude were common. It may be that Buller was right to continue to attempt to save the city rather than wait for Roberts, even if his efforts were clumsy.

While Buller was winning his ponderous way into Ladysmith, Roberts and Kitchener were taking control of the rest of the war and planning the last conventional campaign. Their first step was to reorganize transport, which had always been provided by individual regiments. The new commanders put the bulk of transport equipment and personnel into a unified pool from which unit commanders were to draw as needed. Logically it made sense for a 'modern' army's transport to be centrally structured. After all, the Boer War required Britain's largest expeditionary force to that date, and supply lines were often very long. The old system, no matter how well it had served Wellington, was due for an overhaul. Unfortunately, initially the changes caused confusion. Soldiers, dependent on established doctrine for victory, tend to become rigid and mistrustful of innovation. This tendency, vital in maintaining discipline in life-threatening situations, was intensified by a reverence for tradition that was particularly strong in the British Army. Therefore, it proved very difficult to alter long-established practices, particularly during a major conflict. Roberts and Kitchener were tenacious enough to force their reforms through, and eventually they were successful. Logistical difficulties lingered in South Africa, however, and the British remained too dependent on the railways for much of the war.

In February 1900 Roberts was ready. He gathered a force of more than 25,000 men, about one-third mounted, at Methuen's base facing Magersfontein. Although the British establishment had reached 180,000 in South Africa, there was concern that he was opening the Cape Colony to invasion because he was pulling so many units into his planned attack. Roberts intended to flank the Boer positions to the east and make a drive on Bloemfontein. It was, for a British commander, a daring move away from rail lines. If successful, he would push on to Pretoria. He had a clear precedent for doing this, but Roberts was making a mistake. Although a geographic objective proved central to this war, that objective was space not places.

Efforts at keeping the new plan quiet were successful, and when the drive began Piet Cronjé, the Boer commander, believed that it represented no more than diversionary attacks by Methuen. He sent Christiaan de Wet to deal with the problem, and word soon came back that the British move was a major offensive. Roberts also knew that politically, though not militarily, the relief of Kimberley was little short of a necessity. General Sir John French with his cavalry was sent in that direction, and on 15 February he made his name with a charge between two hills at Klip's Drift, splitting the Boer lines and opening the way to the city. He was very close to Cronjé's main laager (fortified camp). It was militarily a much more desirable prize than Kimberley, but French did not know its location and following his orders moved on to the city. Although Rhodes and the British garrison and inhabitants came through the siege in reasonable shape – the company warehouses even produced the wherewithal for a real celebration when the relief arrived – at least one observer reported that no black baby survived.

That same day real trouble began to develop in the British rear. Their enormous supply train, struggling across the Riet River at Waterval Drift, was attacked by De Wet. The guard took up a defensive position and help was sent back, but the next day when the British attempted to break out gunfire stampeded the oxen and about half of them charged into Boer lines. Reinforcements were requested, and Roberts had to decide what to do. Ultimately, he abandoned the supply train, and put his troops on half rations. He was thus able to save time and continue his offensive, but the men paid in terms of stamina because it took a number of weeks to make good the losses. With French at Kimberley and having taken Jacobsdal, Roberts continued his flank drive, and Methuen opened a renewed push at Magersfontein. Cronjé was faced with potential disaster.

Startled by both the size and mobility of the new offensive, Cronjé was slow to react. Eventually, he fell back to the east – passing undetected within 3 miles of French's lines – but his force did not move quickly. Significant numbers of horses had been lost and many burghers's families had joined them during the siege. For once it was a Boer column that was dangerously slowed by ox wagons and baggage. Apparently thinking that Kimberley was the main objective of the British, Cronjé moved away in a direct line to Bloemfontein, but this put him in the line of Roberts's intended march. On 16 February French, whose men had worn themselves and their horses out fruitlessly chasing rear guard units around Kimberley, received orders to cut off Cronjé, who was known to be moving eastward along the Modder River. Although he was able to mount only about 1,200 troopers, on 18 February French caught the Boers at Paardeberg Drift, surprising them by opening fire with field artillery. The tired and outnumbered cavalry was fortunate that the Boers were too confused to organize a concerted attack, for the way to escape would have almost certainly been opened.

French held his ground, however, and Kitchener – Roberts was delayed by a brief illness – rushed infantry to Paardeberg to trap Cronjé's force. By the rather elaborate rules of seniority in the British Army, the ranking officer present was Lieutenant-General Sir Thomas Kelly-Kenny, and he planned to shell the Boers into surrender. Kitchener was determined to inflict a dramatic defeat on the enemy and had a letter from Roberts saying that he wanted Kitchener's orders taken as his own. Kelly-Kenny accepted this but without enthusiasm, and he has been accused of letting this influence his performance. Kitchener ordered frontal assaults against the Boer laager, but he was trying to conduct a battle using the very limited, sometimes resentful, staffs of units with which he had never worked before. The result was a series of unco-ordinated attacks that the Boers were able to stop. Without communications, Kitchener rushed about the battlefield, often issuing incomplete orders to individual units. Major-General Horace Smith-Dorrien was told to take his brigade and a battery of artillery across the river and establish a position. As the river was in flood and the Boers controlled the only visible drift, he asked about crossing and was informed Kitchener expected him to find a way. He did, but then was given no directions about what to do next. The more attacks failed the more furious Kitchener became. He began to imply that unit failure reflected personal failure of commanders. Colonel Ormelie Hannay of the mounted infantry was so outraged at what he regarded as personal insult that he led fifty men in a suicidal charge succeeding in personally breeching Boer lines before being shot off his horse. The overall result was the bloodiest single day of the war for the British and Cronjé's laager was not taken.

Appeals for aid for Cronjé were unheeded except by the indomitable Christiaan de Wet, who seized a hill in the midst of the British lines from which to cover a breakout. To his intense frustration, Cronjé refused to move, even after some small groups got away, and De Wet had to withdraw. Roberts arrived and cancelled Kitchener's plans to renew the attacks. The British settled down to blast the Boers out of the laager. Although this worked, it meant some ten days in place with the troops getting their water from the polluted Modder. The result for the British, weakened by being on half rations, was a raging epidemic of typhoid (then called enteric) fever. The disease was far and away the greatest single cause of casualties in the entire war. On 27 February – Majuba Day – Cronjé surrendered. Dressed in scruffy civilian clothes and accompanied by his wife, Cronjé met Roberts, who wore neat but unadorned khaki, and was invited to lunch. It is one of the lingering images of the war. The symbolism of the day – revenge for the British and humiliation for the Boers – is also notable.

Kitchener had been sent from Paardeberg to protect rail lines to the west. These had been left only screened, and Koos De la Rey was in position to cut them thus stranding Roberts's whole force on the veld. Fortunately, many of the commandos in the western theatre were called to the defence of Bloemfontein and supplies continued to flow. Slowed by such logistical matters and typhoid, Roberts nonetheless continued his push toward Bloemfontein, while Buller, reinforced by Ladysmith's garrison, moved slowly out of Natal.

Staggered but not broken, the Boers – 6,000 men led by De Wet – took a defensive position at Popular Grove. As he learned of the position, Roberts developed a good plan of attack. He intended to envelop his foe, sending infantry forces around one side and French's cavalry on a 17-mile encircling ride on the other. It had the potential for creating a decisive defeat, possibly enough to end the war. It failed because the cavalry did not close the gap. French blamed exhausted horses, but many have charged him with delaying out of personal pique. Roberts had mistakenly dressed the cavalryman down for excessive use of feed, and French had not taken it well. Whatever the cause, the burghers had an escape route and, realizing their danger, used it without even making much of a fight.

Annoyed, but not distracted, Roberts pushed on to Bloemfontein, which he entered on 13 March. Over the next few weeks the tide of war seemed to have turned into a British flood. On 17 May a flying column relieved Mafeking, prompting several days of riotous celebration in Britain. Eleven days later the Orange Free State was annexed and renamed the Orange River Colony, and three days later Johannesburg fell. In less than a week Pretoria was also in British hands. In June and July Roberts pushed north-east pursuing the remaining large bodies of Boer troops in the Brandwater Basin. Roberts then declared victory, and prepared to return to Britain and his rewards, which were to include an earldom and a grant of £100,000 from Parliament. He left Kitchener to 'mop-up' and arrange the final peace, which London insisted had to start with unconditional surrender. Unfortunately, Roberts misunderstood what had happened. In his drive on their capitals, he had only brushed aside Boer defenders, leaving them in the field under arms. He regarded them as defeated, but they did not agree. Inspired particularly by De Wet, the commandos were launching a new phase of the war. They were starting to introduce the world to the modern concept of guerrilla fighting, and, despite Roberts's confidence, the war in South Africa had some eighteen months to run.

FIVE

Kitchener's Campaign

With the taking of the capitals of the South African Republic and the Orange Free State, the British, including Lord Roberts, believed that the war was won. Roberts had carried on his campaign for several months, pursuing large contingents in the Brandwater Basin. Success was quite limited. Although Marthinus Prinsloo surrendered on 31 July 1900 with more than 4,000 men, a number of commandos and more importantly General Christiaan de Wet and President Marthinus Steyn of the Free State managed to elude capture and slip over the mountains. They were determined to continue the war and increasingly aware of the potential for a new style of conflict. De Wet, a farmer whose parents had been part of the Great Trek and who had served in the First Boer War, became the key man in developing the guerrilla tactics that were to confound the British for the next year and a half. De Wet was personally outraged at being called a guerrilla and insisted that he was conducting formal military campaigns for a valid, if peripatetic, government. He interpreted guerrilla to mean rebel or at least resister after conquest was complete, but his tactics would be labelled guerrilla today.

The keys to the new tactics were speed and elusiveness. De Wet had already argued forcefully that commandos had to reduce their baggage, but now he insisted, even if it meant relieving elected officers of their commands if they resisted. This required that personal wagons be left behind. It seems a sensible and fairly obvious idea, but wagons were more than possessions to Boers. They were the symbols of the Great Trek that had brought their ancestors to new homes. They were vital farm equipment and provided a degree of both personal and economic independence. They were expensive and not easily replaced. Nonetheless, De Wet insisted that commandos had to move quickly and rapidly, and although when possible a few supply wagons might be included, a baggage train had to go. Wagons were not the only encumbrance eliminated, for by mid-1900 commandos were even giving up artillery – they often had no ammunition for it anyway.

The British had ample warning of this new style of warfare. Having regrouped after his troops fled from

Popular Grove, De Wet decided to take the Bloemfontein waterworks at Sanna's Post, to which only about 200 guards had been assigned. As he moved into position, he discovered that Brigadier-General R.G. Broadwood was moving 1,800 cavalrymen from Thaba Nchu to Bloemfontein and would pass right by Sanna's Post. De Wet had about 1,600 men, a few field pieces and a machine-gun. He decided that despite being outnumbered, he could not only destroy the waterworks but actually capture Broadwood's force. Telling no one what he was planning – a security policy he adopted for the rest of the war – he positioned most of his men across from Sanna's Post, under the command of his brother, Piet. He took a few hundred men a short distance down the river toward Bloemfontein, hiding them in a valley that was on the most direct route to the city.

On the morning of 31 March 1900 the British, who had done no patrolling, got their call to breakfast from Boer artillery. The surprise was complete. Broadwood assumed that De Wet's band was a much larger enemy force which he believed to be in the area. He hastily broke camp and headed for Bloemfontein. As wagons and men entered De Wet's valley slowing to cross the drift there, they were met by orders of 'Hands-Up!'. De Wet's hope of taking the entire lot was frustrated because his men failed to take enough initiative about moving captured men and equipment out of the way. The process slowed down, and in the confusion an artillery officer slipped away to warn his commander. A cavalry officer also saw that something was wrong and turned his unit back. The British rallied, although efforts to shell Boer positions resulted mostly in casualties among the brave gunners, for without howitzers even short-range fire had little effect on the well-entrenched Boers. Broadwood eventually extracted most of his men and equipment and was able to move off toward Bloemfontein with the Boers nipping at his heels.

The results of the fight at Sanna's Post were 159 British killed or wounded, 421 captured and an increase in the already serious typhoid epidemic resulting from the loss of a clean water supply for some weeks. De Wet reported losing three dead and five wounded and capturing most of a battery of field pieces, as well as eighty-three wagons loaded with supplies. Although reinforced, De Wet did not have the mass to stage a large-scale battle. He rode away to Dewetsdorp (named for his father) where he found another target and won another victory, taking a further 470 prisoners. The tactical pattern of quick strikes at available targets and disengaging before the British numerical superiority could be brought to bear was established.

The victories at Sanna's Post and Dewetsdorp provided just the fillip Boer morale needed. The loss of Bloemfontein and the obvious inability to stop Roberts from going on to Pretoria had led many to assume regretfully that the war was lost. More and more Boers accepted Roberts's offer of amnesty in return for the surrender of weapons and the signing of a loyalty oath. The British took no official notice that many of the weapons surrendered were obsolete hunting pieces rather than the modern Mausers that had been used in combat. Those who took the loyalty oath were expected to resume civilian life. The retention of military weapons suggests that not all intended to do so, and those that did were quickly under pressure from neighbours who denounced them as cowardly traitors. In addition, as British pressure grew to stop support for commandos in the field, many of the 'hands-uppers', as the Boers called them, began to feel that official promises of a return to normality were being broken. Pulling burghers back into military action became increasingly easy.

Without fixed governments – the Orange Free State was annexed on 28 May 1900 and the South African Republic on 3 September – logistics were a problem. The stripped down commandos, however, needed relatively little support. Almost every farm was a source of food, intelligence and sometimes remounts. Captured supplies were also a major resource. By mid-1900 ammunition for Mausers was in increasingly short supply and more and more burghers were carrying captured Lee-Metfords. Reportedly, burghers could glean significant numbers of cartridges by following the path of a British column and, of course, every captured or killed Tommy was stripped of his ammunition. Railways were obvious targets, and if a train were captured large amounts of supplies could be taken. When possible the extra was carried away and hidden, but when not, it was burned. The British countered by destroying Boer sources of supply, and by 1901 commandos were stripping prisoners of their clothing to replace the ragged remains of their own clothing. As Rayne Kruger points out, by the end of the war the British taxpayer was funding both sides. The wearing of British clothes was taken by Kitchener as a serious violation of the rules of war because the soldiers of one army are not supposed to wear the uniform of the other. He maintained that it was being done to hoodwink his forces into mistaking commandos for British units. Boers, such as Jan Smuts, whose commando was particularly known for the practice, defended their actions as simply a matter of necessity. Their country was ravaged and they were, sometimes almost literally, naked. It was one more source of bitterness between the two sides.

For the British the guerrilla conflict was the death of a thousand cuts. No small unit seemed safe and catching commandos was almost impossible. Based on Roberts's assertion that the war was at an end, the Army Remount Department, never known for its efficiency, started reducing the number of animals obtained. Units whose enlistments expired were sent home. Thus as they became aware that there was still fighting to be done, the British had to rush green troops and poorly broken horses to South Africa. One of Roberts's legacies to Kitchener was an army that had to relearn many lessons. Another was methods of repression that took the conflict a significant way into the practice of total war that was to dominate the new century, until fear of nuclear holocaust forced the world's belligerents back to limited conflicts.

The new methods began with Roberts's order to burn the farms in a 10-mile radius of attacks on railways. There was precedent for such action from the Franco-Prussian War, when the Germans used similar methods to stop *franc-tireurs* (free fighters).

The theory was that a commando could not operate in the area without at least the knowledge, if not active co-operation, of the local residents. Over the following months this policy was expanded, and the British began to burn the farms and crops and kill the livestock of those who actively resisted, though initially the mere fact that a man was away on commando was not enough to order the destruction of his farm. The standards blurred as the guerrilla campaigns continued, and the destruction of farms became, supposedly, a matter of striking at the enemy's logistical system – a legitimate military target. It was also the modern total war objective of breaking the enemy people's will to fight. The devastation of the infrastructure of the Boer states (now officially colonies) was enormous. The bitterness of the people lingers to the present.

The ruination of farms created a new problem – refugees. The families who lived on the burned farms were often forced to grab what possessions they could carry and flee onto the veld. Initially, the British decided that they should be sent to join their menfolk with the commandos. This was a military decision to put additional pressure on the enemy's logistics, but such blatant use of civilians, including children, resulted in angry outcries both in South Africa and Britain. Something else had to be done.

The British had already begun to create refugee camps for burghers and their families who had initially supported Britain or who had changed sides during the struggle. Moving such people to camps was intended to protect them from harassment by their neighbours, who regarded them as traitors. These camps were quickly expanded to accommodate families from burned farms and soon came to be called concentration camps. By August 1901 there were reportedly 74,000 women and children in some fifty camps; by the end of the war the total was 120,000.

It was a mistake to leave the organization and running of such camps to the military, a policy that was later changed. Operation of facilities for civilians, especially women and children, was not part of Army training. Worse, staff were selected from the locally available pool, thereby reducing the likelihood that those running the camps would have any knowledge of, let alone expertise in, what they were being asked to do. Sites for the camps were often picked on the basis of availability of transportation rather than adequate supplies of water and appropriate drainage. Rations were not necessarily of the best quality, perhaps adequate for soldiers on campaign but not for growing children. Many of these problems were worsened by intransigence and lack of education on the part of the inmates. The Boer women did not trust and so did not listen to the British, even to doctors. They employed folk remedies rather than reporting to the infirmaries and sometimes ignored basic sanitary rules as if they were still living in very low density on the veld. This combination of factors resulted in terrible epidemics of typhoid, measles and other infectious diseases. At its peak, in October 1901, the death rate rose to 344 per 1,000. After the transfer of the camps to civilian control, which took place on 1 March 1901 in the Transvaal and 1 November in the Orange River Colony, the rate declined dramatically to 160 per 1,000 in January 1902, and 20 per 1,000 in May 1902.

Initially, the camps were, if not strictly speaking secret, at least not publicized. Roberts was able to go home and escape any blame, although he initiated the policy. Kitchener expanded them, but there is no record of his ever visiting one. The camps became highly controversial because of the crusade of a Quaker spinster named Emily Hobhouse, who was concerned about the suffering of those she regarded as innocents. From January to April 1901 Hobhouse was in South Africa visiting camps and talking to inmates. To say she was appalled would be an understatement of epic proportions. She returned to England, where she produced a series of pamphlets and made numerous public appearances denouncing the camps and accusing the authorities of both callousness and deliberate cruelty. While the charges may have been extreme, they were politically potent and stirred opposition to the war, already a problem for the British government. To counter these effects and calm public opinion, Millicent Fawcett, a moderate suffragette, was appointed to head a Women's Commission and conduct an official investigation of the situation.

The Women's Commission, which included a female physician, was perhaps the first entirely female body officially to represent the government of Great Britain. The ladies went to South Africa and made an inspection tour of the camps. Although denounced by Hobhouse and her supporters as a whitewash, their report identified numerous problems. For instance, at Howich, scarlet fever cases were not isolated, and there were, for 4,900 inmates, only 65 latrine pails for women and 23 for men. At Merebank, 5,154 people shared a total of fourteen baths. Such conditions were widespread and when revealed by an establishment source, hastened the hand-over to civilian control. When Hobhouse, who did grudgingly admit that there had been some improvement in camp life, attempted to return to South Africa, Kitchener refused her entry. Hobhouse protested vigorously and even claimed she needed to land for reasons of health, but the general was not swayed by such efforts to turn the gender double standard against him. Hobhouse was put on a ship leaving for England. She continued her public relations effort, and the issue, while it became less of a *cause célèbre*, remained troublesome.

Although there are some accounts that suggest that Boers were actually glad to have their dependants cared for during the war, these seem to be from people who took the British side politically. Boer accounts generally emphasized the suffering of the inmates and blamed the British authorities. During the last year of the war, De Wet reported that boys of ten and younger joined his commando, at risk to life and limb, to avoid being sent to a camp. The vast majority of comments from South Africa, then and now, describe the camps as barbarous and blame the British authorities for every injury.

There were also camps for non-whites, refugees and former servants of white inmates. Anecdotal evidence suggests these were every bit as bad, probably much worse than those for whites. Regrettably, these camps were never visited by English campaigners, and information about them is scarce. Estimates of deaths among non-white inmates range from 7,000 to more than 13,000. The role and problems of blacks in the supposedly white Boer War have only recently come under significant scrutiny. In addition to their service as scouts, auxiliaries and labourers, performed in all the besieged cities and on the lines of supply, blacks were sometimes openly part of the military effort. For instance, the Kgatla, under their shrewd ruler Linchwe I, fought a campaign on behalf of the British to defend the border of Bechuanaland against Boer incursion. Although their supposed allies refused most of their requests for weapons, they were successful, and while in the end they did not gain all of the territory they had expected, their herds were greatly augmented. Black Africans often took advantage of the war to replace cattle recently lost to the rinderpest, although the disease continued to spread, but on the whole they were poorly rewarded for their efforts in the conflict. In Calvinia, Namaqualand, Abraham Esau, a coloured (the term for those of mixed race), angered at mistreatment by Afrikaners, organized resistance and co-operated with British intelligence. Taken by the Boers, he was repeatedly beaten in a vain attempt to extract a confession. Then he was flogged for speaking against the Boers. Finally, clapped in leg-irons he was dragged several miles behind a horse, beaten again and finally executed. Although his story became a convenient example for the British to use in denouncing the Boers, there does not seem to have been any official recognition of his sacrifice for the British cause.

Militarily the British situation was not initially improved by efforts to control the Boer population. President Steyn was not far from being right when he asserted that the Boers were better off in August 1901 than they had been a year earlier. Commandos ranged widely in the Cape Colony, and in the former Boer states Kitchener's jurisdiction was limited to the range of his guns. Even law and order was generally maintained by the landdrosts (district magistrates) appointed by the republics. Therefore, in addition to burning farms and shipping dependants off to concentration camps, Kitchener had to develop military counters to the guerrilla tactics. He increased the number of mounted troops in his command and tried to use the added mobility to pursue the commandos. His cavalry, however, could rarely match the Boers. When the British got close, the Boers would leave a rear guard of men whose horses were the least exhausted. This guard would pick a defendable hill and fire on the advancing British. The response, if done by the book, was to bring guns forward, shell the enemy position and then attack. Typically, this took several hours, and the Boer guard slipped away rather than be shelled. The result was that the commando had time to escape. Pursuing the Boers, who had greatly superior knowledge of the land, excellent scouts such as Danie Theron and Gideon Scheepers, and friends on all sides, was unlikely to produce a quick victory. The British needed a means to control their foe's freedom to move.

Kitchener saw potential in barbed-wire fencing that was being used to establish defendable lines ranging out from some towns. He began to build such fences to literally divide the country into sections. Every few hundred yards there was a blockhouse. Construction was initially a problem, but Army engineers quickly realized that an adequate blockhouse could be built from two concentric circles of corrugated iron by filling the space between with rocks and dirt. Once a conical roof of the same material was added and some loopholes cut, the structure was ready to house seven or eight soldiers. Commonly, a blockhouse unit also had a few blacks as servants and armed scouts. Ultimately, there were some 5,000 miles of fence and 10,000 blockhouses built.

Kitchener's plan was to do sweeps with columns of cavalry and mounted infantry to trap commandos against the wire. If burghers tried to cross the lines, they would come under fire from the blockhouses (fences were built at angles so that the blockhouses would not be in one another's lines of fire) and the pursuers alerted. Although the elusive commandos managed again and again to slip through these barriers, attrition was on the side of the British. Commandos had few replacements and so casualties meant reduced forces. Prisoners were commonly sent out of the country to such places as St Helena, Ceylon and Bermuda. By this point in the war, commandos had no means to keep prisoners and customarily released them after a short time. Thus a British soldier taken by the Boers was likely to be back in action in a few days. It is a testimonial to the Boer belief in their ideals – they were fighting for their freedom and independence – that month after month, often knowing that their families were in camps ravaged by epidemics, they fought on. The system succeeded only by wearing the Boers down. The British made three massive efforts to trap De Wet – the Great De Wet hunts – and failed. Although the Boers were being exhausted, it is notable that when the final peace negotiations began Jan Smuts had to be recalled from the far south-western part of Cape Colony where his commando was besieging the copper mining centre of O'okiep.

SIX

The Pro-Boer Agitation

The military elements that make the Boer War and the American war in Vietnam similar have often been identified. A great power attacked a small nation. Conventional military forces were confounded by guerrillas. The superior firepower failed due to the lack of targets. Ill-advised efforts to force the population into cooperation were attempted. The ideological elements were also similar. Like the Vietnamese, the Boers were inspired by a sense of nationalism. They were fighting for freedom and independence and were willing to sacrifice a great deal. But, unlike the Vietnamese, once the war started the Boers could not get significant material aid from outside and they did not have an independent state into which they could withdraw for sanctuary. This, of course, meant that the Boers could be worn down more rapidly and more surely than the Vietnamese.

There was another ideological similarity. Within the great power, public opinion divided and an anti-war movement arose. In both cases it caused significant social turmoil and had long-term political results. The American anti-war effort had more influence in causing peace than did the British. The American war lasted longer and was for most of the time based on conscription, which led to a more extensive involvement of youth in the opposition to it than would have been the case if such opposition were merely a matter of principle. In each movement principle did matter, however. Both movements were also mixed in method and sometimes conducted via rude comment and public demonstration. Perhaps David Lloyd George's reference to the supporters of the war in South Africa as 'Union Jackasses' may stand as example for both.

In addition to public meetings, the pro-Boers, as opponents of the war came to be known, had three main forums. The press, an obvious vehicle for attempting to shape public opinion, was initially mostly hostile. The only major, respected paper that supported their view for the first year of the war was the *Manchester Guardian*, which had long been known for its liberal editorial position. Its impact within the middle-class business community was substantial, but it did not reach London until mid-morning. Thus establishment papers – *The Times* was pro-government from first shot to last – could reach decision-makers with news and interpretation first. This remained a problem until January 1901, when the pro-Boers gained control of the *Daily News*.

Another major means of reaching people was pamphlets. Although reduced by the advent of the penny press in the second half of the nineteenth century, pamphleteering was a venerable English tradition going back to the Civil War. The outpouring of pamphlets concerning the Boer War was enormous, running into the thousands. Pamphlets on both sides ranged from the most scurrilous demagogism to serious comment, but misrepresentation was much more common on the pro-government side.

Finally, there was opportunity in parliamentary debate for the pro-Boers to make their case. The Liberal Party, to which virtually all of them belonged (Kier Hardie's Labour Representation Committee was firmly against the war but was too small to be a meaningful part of the movement), was split roughly into thirds. The Liberal-Imperialists (Lib Imps, or Limps to those who disliked them) supported the government. Their ranks included most of the rising stars of Liberalism such as H.H. Asquith, Sir Edward Grey and R.B. Haldane. The radical wing, however, adopted the pro-Boer position and had well-established leaders such as Sir William Harcourt and John Morley, and in David Lloyd George a rising star of its own. Between the two extremes was a group of moderates including the party leader, Sir Henry Campbell-Bannerman, who had to walk a narrow path to avoid losing one side or the other.

The pro-Boers had two major organizations through which protests were mounted. One, the South African Conciliation Committee, had grown out of the Transvaal Independence Association, founded in 1881 to seek repeal of the 1877 annexation. It was comparatively conservative and inclined to urge terms and compromises that might bring the war to an acceptable conclusion. At the beginning, its members tended to regard other pro-Boers as a bit extreme. The other group was the Stop the War Committee, which appeared immediately after hostilities began. As its name suggests, this organization favoured an immediate end to hostilities. Its positions tended to be expressed emotionally and vigorously. Its best-known member was the journalist W.T. Stead, whose *Review of Reviews* had clearly established him as a leader of the more extreme liberal factions. In the long-run, the differences between the two groups tended to be more matters of attitude and rhetoric than issues, and by the end it became difficult to tell them apart.

Agitation began in the months before the declaration of war in October 1899 in the hope of preventing hostilities, and continued into the aftermath of the conflict.

The pro-Boers quickly rose to the attack. They asserted that the Uitlanders had little to complain about, compared to those concerned with suffrage in Great Britain, and since they had been able to make great profits, war seemed an extreme means of redress. Stead compared the government's handling of the outbreak to the Dreyfus case in terms of misrepresentation and cover ups, and John Burns, who would later be a major figure in the Labour Party, pointed out that the vigour of a pro-war speech in Parliament seemed directly proportional to the maker's number of shares in South African enterprises. Race was a common theme. The war was frequently depicted as serving the interest of Jewish bankers and businessmen, though just how the religious/ethnic characteristics of the culpable capitalists was relevant was universally ignored. Such financiers were generally accused of wanting cheap black labour which would, of course, drive down the wages of whites. Occasionally, other concerns about the situation of blacks were expressed, but perhaps at least in part because the other side pointed out the failings of the British in such matters, the fate of black Africans was not a major theme for the pro-Boers.

Anti-war meetings were sometimes disrupted. The opposition ran from heckling to rioting. Lloyd George sneered at the calls to revenge Majuba noting that the Army had suffered a series of Majubas in the effort. The war's object, he said, had become greed for annexation. The opponents of the pro-Boers saw such extremes as comfort for the enemy if not outright treason. In the beginning the anti-war view was not popular, and reports of police failing to protect its proponents became increasingly common. Ultimately, this gave the pro-Boers a new issue: free speech. They appealed to the traditional rights of Englishmen to speak out even if their views were not popular, and also argued that the assertion that the war was intended to defend the rights of Uitlanders was hard to sustain if the right of free speech were suppressed at home. This gave Campbell-Bannerman the chance to speak on behalf of the pro-Boers without having to endorse their position on the war. The politically astute Scotsman did so, leaving himself in reasonably good stead with both wings of his party.

Early in 1900 the tide of war seemed to be turning. Robert's victory at Paardeberg on 18 February fed popular enthusiasm, and among numerous outbreaks of violence John Burns had to face down a mob that broke his windows and threatened more. With the fall of Bloemfontein and Pretoria, final victory seemed at hand, and Lord Salisbury, Prime Minister and head of the Conservative and Unionist Party, urged on by Joseph Chamberlain, saw an opportunity. His government, elected in 1895, was nearing the end of its constitutional term and showing some signs of reduced popularity – its majority had fallen from 152 to 128. An appeal to patriotism might just give it a new lease on life. He called what became the first 'khaki election' in British history. The Boer War was the first occasion in the era of general male suffrage that such a nationalistic election campaign was a realistic possibility. Such appeals are always condemned for both idealistic and self-serving reasons. Lloyd George found this one appalling, but did very much the same thing in 1918. Chamberlain, however, announced that a seat lost to the government was a seat gained by the Boers. He was accused of saying 'sold to the Boers', but that seems to have been the result of a telegrapher's erroneous transcription. Such slogans, however, asserting that opposing the government was supporting the Boers, were common during the election. Unionist pamphlets expanded the charge of treason from those who had supported the Transvaal's interests before the war to opponents of continuing it. The vituperativeness reached the point where Unionists made no distinction among 'pro-Boer', 'Liberal' and 'traitor' as epithets. The Liberal-Imperialists thought such a distinction was called for, and tended to move away from the pro-war advocates.

Ironically enough, the election did not do the government much good. Although its majority in popular vote grew by almost 20 per cent, its net gain in seats was only three. On the whole, the Liberals could claim to have held their own, but hardly to have gained much. Their party was still too split to really mount any unified campaign regarding the war, and Campbell-Bannerman felt compelled to make overtures to Lord Rosebery, the retired party leader and favourite of Liberal-Imperialists. Rosebery did not return to active politics, but faced with the possibility of declining influence, the pro-Boers regrouped. There was concern that strident voices such as Stead's and Lloyd George's had cost them politically and there was some question about how to proceed with the anti-war campaign. Campbell-Bannerman did adopt a more critical stance concerning Chamberlain and his version of imperialism and questioned the insistence on unconditional surrender, but he was careful not to appear openly pro-Boer or unpatriotic. At this time, a new and potent issue emerged.

In South Africa Lord Roberts had begun his policy of burning farms and moving Boer women and children to concentration camps. As word of this strategy reached Britain, the pro-Boers quickly seized on it as a new example of the government's wickedness and demanded more access to information about what was going on. Furthermore, appeals for aid for innocents interned in the camps could be apolitical and yet draw the uncommitted into the anti-war effort. For the first time there was a clear politicization of women, and because of their experience in the struggle for suffrage, feminist leaders had some knowledge of how to be an effective pressure group. The South African Women and Children Distress Fund was created to provide a means of helping camp inmates. For the Liberal Party, the result was an easing of its division over the war. On 27 February 1901 the National Liberal Federation called for an end to the war on terms that allowed the Boers some self-government. A few days later, Campbell-Bannerman made a speech strong enough in support of the Boers that it was condemned as supporting the enemy. In South Africa, tentative peace talks between Louis Botha and Lord Kitchener collapsed over the issue of treatment of Cape Dutch supporters of the Boers. Kitchener was willing to grant them amnesty as Botha wanted, but Milner insisted on punishing them as traitors. The Liberals, however, assumed that the problem was the government's insistence on unconditional surrender. That assumption helped consolidate opposition to the war on grounds that it continued due to London's rigidity.

The anti-war campaign received an enormous boost in mid-1901 with the reports of Emily Hobhouse, who returned from visiting the concentration camps to portray them as little less than charnel houses. Her views were spread far and wide by the South African Women and Children Distress Fund, which published her reports and letters as pamphlets and sponsored public meetings where she spoke. As this part of the campaign grew more intense, the involvement of women increased. The Women's Liberal Federation expanded its position from the support of pro-suffrage parliamentary candidates to attacking the demand for unconditional surrender and the involvement of women and children in the conduct of the war. Campbell-Bannerman had a long meeting with Hobhouse and was left personally outraged at what his country was doing. He soon turned his feelings to political advantage. On 14 June 1901 he made a speech in which, mocking the remark of St John Brodrick, the Secretary of State for War, that 'war is war', he asserted 'When is a war not a war? When it is carried on by methods of barbarism in South Africa.'

Although denounced as an unpatriotic attack on soldiers serving in South Africa rather than on the overall conduct of the war, the phrase 'methods of barbarism' became the new rallying cry of a revitalized and more militant pro-Boer movement. It appears that pro-Boers were now ready to incite violence by the use of deliberately inflammatory language and to retaliate physically against even mild opposition. The other side did not, however, back down. Some of Hobhouse's meetings were cancelled from fear of violence, but she reportedly held some twenty-three from late June to the end of July 1901. She and her supporters offered disputed but telling statistics to support the emotional appeals. For instance, one report asserted that of some 54,326 white children in the camps, 1,954 died in September 1901 – far from the worst month. Faced with such figures, and with the war moving into its third year, Nonconformist churches began to join the opposition. The war was decried as national sin, and a manifesto attacking it attracted the signatures of more than 5,000 ministers by late October.

The Liberal Party began to associate itself more and more with the anti-war position, though the Liberal-Imperialists held their ground. Casualty and expense figures provided added fodder for the rhetoric. According to Sir Robert Reid, Liberal MP for Dumfries, 17,000 to 18,000 were dead, and if that were not enough, the national debt had risen by a quarter. Censorship was preventing the people from knowing what was really happening. Campbell-Bannerman expanded his attacks on methods of barbarism, and was increasingly criticized along with his party for encouraging the Boers to continue their struggle. By the end of 1901 opinions were changing. Even Lord Rosebery, an imperialist and by no stretch of the imagination a pro-Boer, called for negotiations in South Africa and firmly rejected the idea that Liberal criticisms had prolonged the war.

Perhaps the most dramatic and militant part of the anti-war effort in the last year of the war came from David Lloyd George, who moved himself into national prominence through a series of peace meetings. Beginning in Wales, his home base, Lloyd George revisited many of the objections to the causes and goals of the war, while pouring purple prose into the emotional campaign about the methods used to fight it. On 19 December 1901 Lloyd George took his campaign to Birmingham,

Chamberlain's home town, where he remained very popular. Despite hecklers in the audience, Lloyd George made some prepared remarks, mostly a reply to Rosebery's recent comments, but before he could move on to expressing his fiery anti-war ideas, a rock came through the front window of the town hall followed by a mob intending to get the traitor. Fortunately, the police were at hand and, although perhaps a dozen were injured in the ensuing riot, they managed to spirit Lloyd George away in a constable's uniform. Chamberlain, asked for comment, merely deplored the damage to the venerable town hall.

By early 1902 the war was clearly winding down. The commandos were exhausted and Kitchener's net of barbed wire fences and blockhouses was increasingly hard to avoid. Negotiations began early in the year and a treaty was signed in April. The pro-Boers took some credit – probably more than they deserved. Campbell-Bannerman had won respect as a politician at home and as a decent man who might make more generous arrangements later among the Boers. The government gained little politically. Chamberlain churlishly continued to denounce the pro-Boers for prolonging the war by making the enemy think that a friendlier government might take power in London if enough time were allowed.

Few, however, seem to have believed that men like Botha and De Wet were much influenced by political debate in London. The Unionist government was soon out of office, and late in 1905 Campbell-Bannerman became Prime Minister. After being confirmed by an election, he moved to restore self-government to the Transvaal. His ability to reach an accommodation that kept South Africa satisfied within the Empire does seem to have been enhanced by the Afrikaner sense that he had opposed the most hated elements in the conduct of the war. Perhaps the pro-Boers had not done so badly after all.

SEVEN

Peace

The first serious peace talks were between Louis Botha and Lord Kitchener at the end of February 1901. Through the good offices of Botha's wife, the two generals met at Middleburg. They found each other congenial and were photographed together. They discussed a number of issues starting with grievances in the conduct of the war. Botha, for instance, raised the Boer concern that the British were arming natives while Kitchener expressed his outrage that burghers were wearing British uniforms. The significant talk, however, was of peace terms. The major terms eventually proposed were as follows:

- the former republics be Crown colonies with self-government to be granted when possible
- the republics's debts be paid up to £1,000,000
- Dutch and English be used in schools and courts
- burghers and Cape rebels be granted amnesty, though the rebels were to be disfranchised

- British aid be given to help with reconstruction
- prisoners be promptly returned
- blacks not to be given the franchise before the colonies had self-government.

These terms were not acceptable in London, and Chamberlain replied to Kitchener and Milner, whose comments had been added before the document was dispatched. Particular objections were raised to granting amnesty to colonial rebels, whom Milner demanded be treated as traitors, and to the failure to assure rights for blacks. Although he maintained that blacks's rights should be limited, Chamberlain said that a peace that did not ensure that such rights were equal to those in the Cape Colony would be 'shameful'. On the Boer side, President Steyn of the Free State was outraged that the meeting was even held. At the time, the Middleburg talks seemed of little moment, but when peace was actually made, the terms discussed there became the basis for the negotiation.

By early 1902 the war, which seemed interminable to people on both sides, was actually winding down. Kitchener's tactics were paying off. In Cape Colony there were about 3,000 invaders and rebels, but it was clear there would be no general rebellion. The southern parts of the former Orange Free State were essentially pacified, but in the north the Boers were still capable of causing trouble. The Eastern and South-eastern Transvaal were mostly under control, though several commandos and most importantly Louis Botha were still active. In the western region, Koos De la Rey with 5,000 men led the strongest of the remaining Boer forces. De la Rey had battered a column led by Lieutenant-Colonel Kekewich on 30 September 1901 at Moedwil. Then at Yzer Spriut on 24 February 1902 he had captured a wagon convoy, taking a substantial amount of supplies. Two weeks later, on 7 March at Tweebosch, he had virtually destroyed a column led by Lord Methuen, who had done much to restore his reputation since the debacle at Magersfontein. The badly wounded Methuen was captured. A lieutenant-general, His Lordship was the highest-ranking British soldier taken during the war. De la Rey's men, angry over farm burning and the death of their commander's son in a battle with Methuen's forces, wanted him tried and executed. In one of the gestures that gave the Boer War the sobriquet 'Last of the Gentlemen's Wars' De la Rey sent Methuen to the nearest British hospital and forwarded a note of sympathy to his wife. It was his last chance for such an act, for Tweebosch turned out to be the last significant Boer victory.

In March Kitchener moved to destroy De la Rey, the 'Lion of the West'. The fence and blockhouse system in the Western Transvaal was limited. It was a barren region and water sources were so scattered that the lines of fence had to be further apart than in other areas. The increased sophistication of the tactical system, now based on more numerous smaller columns associated in larger formations, was effective, however. The first attempt, launched on 23 March, employed thirteen columns grouped into four larger units, but was largely unsuccessful. It netted only eight burghers killed, 165 prisoners and a few pieces of artillery De la Rey had abandoned to increase his mobility. Kitchener arrived on 26 March in his armoured train, the HMT (His Majesty's Train) *Cobra*, equipped with guns and searchlights.

Aware that the real problem was intelligence, Kitchener brought in Aubrey Wools-Sampson, who had organized a system of local agents in the Eastern Transvaal that had been a very effective help in tracking commandos. Perhaps due to the lack of time, he was of little use in the Western region. On 31 March De la Rey escaped again, this time mauling a unit commanded by Kitchener's brother, Walter. Kitchener, however, stuck to his tactic of brute force, still intending to overwhelm the Boers. He did make a refinement, however. At the suggestion of his generals, he put Lieutenant-General Ian Hamilton in overall charge of the next drive. Having someone on the scene with the authority to coordinate movements of all columns proved valuable.

Hamilton worked out a plan to use three groups of columns that were to start an advance and then double back to trap De la Rey in one of his favourite hideouts. What in the past might have been a fatal error occurred when a message to Kekewich, in command of one force, miscarried and his troops and those of Henry Rawlinson ended up in the same place. In this case, Hamilton was at hand to sort out the confusion, and the error worked to British advantage. Boer scouts had noted the gap in the British ring, a tempting target, but with Hamilton's reorganization, the weak point had become the strongest. Near Roodewal farm a force of about a thousand burghers led by F.J. Potgieter charged, overwhelming a scouting party. It was typical of a new and effective tactic the Boers had developed, based on a sudden cavalry charge with the troopers firing from horseback. It called for surprise and cover, and at Roodewal they had neither. They found themselves riding all out across the open veld into a massed formation of some 2,000 men with artillery support. Although some of the green British troops broke, as Methuen's had at Tweebosch, the formation held and the attack was beaten off. Potgieter with a small group continued to charge until they were all shot off their horses, some within only a few yards of their enemy. Had Hamilton, fearing a counter-attack and faced with awkward terrain, not moved slowly in pursuit he could have surrounded the entire commando. It was the last formal battle of the war.

The battle Roodewal took place on 11 April 1902, the first day of the negotiations that were to result in a treaty. Kitchener had quietly let the Boer leadership know of a Dutch proposal to mediate, and although London had refused, he tacitly hinted that talks might be in order. Arrangements were quickly made, and on 11 April a delegation led by Botha, Smuts, De Wet and Steyn arrived at Pretoria. To Kitchener's amazement, his guests offered to accept what were essentially the terms Kruger had rejected at Bloemfontein almost three years earlier. They even proposed retaining their independence, as though there had been no war. To prevent a complete collapse of the talks, Kitchener sent the proposal to his government, which promptly insisted on unconditional surrender but at the same time allowed a symbolic condition. Milner, who had not been invited to the meeting on 11 April, was told to join the negotiations. His presence indicated that the talks were not just a matter of generals arranging a surrender, but were between represent- atives of His Majesty and a nation if not a government (by British law the Boer governments had been terminated by annexation of the republics). Certainly the burghers regarded themselves as more than rebels in arms, and now perhaps their opponents did too.

Milner was beside himself. By this point in time he was convinced that a few more months of fighting would bring Boer collapse, and British authorities would have unlimited opportunity to remake South Africa. He expected to be the head of that authority. He had already made notable progress on reconstruction. His 'Kindergarten' (a group of talented young aides) was at work seeing to the rebuilding of the infrastructure, most importantly railways, improving the concentration camp situation and getting the gold mines working again. At the price of stricter pass laws and reduced wages for the black workforce, the mines were producing more than a third of the gold that had been mined before the war. The new colonies were actually self- sufficient in revenue. Milner wanted a free hand to build on this foundation, and he feared that Kitchener had lost sight of the fact that it was not the British who needed to make peace. He urged

Chamberlain to make no concessions beyond London's version of the Middleburg terms.

It is not clear what the Boer delegates were thinking. There was little if any likelihood that their proposal would be accepted or even discussed. When they heard the rejection as well as the news of Roodewal, on 14 April, they had no alternative to offer. They announced that their authority did not extend to yielding independence, and asked that the British suggest terms. Although again not expecting a positive result, Kitchener sent the request to London. The response came on 17 April and made it clear that London would go no further than the Middleburg terms. The delegation of burghers then asked for an armistice to consult with representatives overseas and their people. By the latter they meant only those burghers still actively involved in the war. The overseas connection was refused, but Kitchener offered use of railways and the telegraph for consultation with the commandos and then safe passage for a meeting at Vereeniging, south of Pretoria on the Vaal River, in May. Starting four days before that meeting, no commando whose leader was involved would be attacked. It was an unusual arrangement. The Boers were being allowed to hold a private meeting with all the arrangements being made by their enemies.

It was Kitchener's doing, and Milner was right in thinking that the general was ready to negotiate and be done with the war. Kitchener was eager to take up command of the Army in India, quite a prize for a general, and was also concerned about the human, physical and moral cost of the war. He seems to have liked the Boer leaders, much more than he liked the loyalists whom Milner wanted to put into control. He was not inclined to make enormous concessions. He had sanctioned the execution of fifty-one Cape rebels, including the popular leaders Gideon Scheepers and Johannes Lûtter, a group for whom the burghers were determined to get an amnesty. Nonetheless, he was ready to talk about terms.

On 16 May sixty delegates elected by the burghers arrived at Vereeniging. Each of the former republics was represented by thirty men, but only the Transvaal sent any who were not ranking officers or politicians. President Steyn, one of the most zealous advocates of fighting on to the bitter end, was present, but too ill to take an active part. Steyn had been an effective inspiration for most of the war, and his illness must account for a significant part of the success of the negotiations. De Wet had dutifully visited each Free State commando before the meeting, and taken votes in each. The result was an overwhelming majority against yielding independence. When the delegation was told by Schalk Burger, acting President of the Transvaal, that Britain would insist on colonial status, De Wet, who regarded himself bound by the vote, was ready to return to the field. Smuts and J.B. Hertzog, both respected legal advisers to the republican governments, intervened and successfully argued that the delegates could not be committed prior to the negotiations and could vote as their consciences directed. After some discussion, this group elected a negotiating team of Louis Botha, Koos De la Rey and Jan Smuts for the Transvaal, and J.B. Hertzog and Christiaan De Wet for the Orange Free State.

Talks began on 19 May in Pretoria. The Boer team was empowered to discuss terms, but any proposal had to be ratified by the entire delegation. The Boers proposed a scheme involving giving the Rand, some other territory and control of foreign affairs to Britain in return for being left in peace to run their own affairs. This was unacceptable, and Milner was ready to break off the negotiations. Kitchener opened an informal dialogue with Smuts even telling him at one point that within two years a Liberal government was likely to take office in London and mitigate the more onerous parts of any agreement made at Vereeniging. Slowly, despite the reluctance of Milner, the stalemate began to break. A statement that the burghers would disarm and acknowledge the King's sovereignty was written for the delegates to take back to Vereeniging. If it were accepted, details of the settlement would be added.

Finally, Smuts and Hertzog sat down with Milner and his advisors and worked out a draft agreement. The terms were much like those proposed at Middleburg, but although they could get no timetable set for self-government, the Boers won a few additional concessions. Only the leaders of the Cape rebels were to be disfranchised, at first for life but later for a period of five years. No commitments were made regarding blacks except that they would not be given votes until after the colonies were granted self-government. The amount Britain was to pay for Boer war debts was raised from £1,000,000 to £3,000,0000. A separate promise of loans to burghers as well as loyalists was added. The agreement was then sent to the two sides for ratification.

Although Milner urged Chamberlain to stall, hoping to find a way to block acceptance, the treaty was warmly received in London. There was some concern about native rights. The Cabinet recognized that if suffrage were not granted while the British were in control it would never be granted. When told that insisting on protection of those rights would prevent Boer ratification, however, the Cabinet left the clause unchanged, and all of the idealism concerning improvements for natives was forgotten. There was also some concern about the financial arrangements. The amount was acceptable, but it should not look like a gift – bribe might have been a more accurate term. The provision for loans was merged with the war debt payment to give the appearance that only legitimate war debts were involved. The treaty got back to Pretoria on 27 May, and the Boers were told that a prompt yes or no decision was required.

Those favouring peace, led by Louis Botha, had suggested a number of factors that made it necessary. There were serious shortages of horses and food. Women and children with the commandos and alone on the veld were suffering terribly and were now refused entry to the camps. Conditions in the camps, which had improved, were not mentioned, but the tendency to see this as evidence that the fighters liked having their families cared for seems questionable. Comments about the camps in veterans's memoirs are commonly bitter denunciations. It seems more likely that dependants with no place to go were simply the most immediate crisis and thus a better argument. It also had another facet.

There was growing concern among the burghers concerning attacks by blacks. Ten days before the negotiations opened there was an incident at Holkrantz, near Vryheid. A Zulu kraal had been raided and burned by a commando. Women and children had been driven out and many cattle taken. The local chief, Sikobobo, had protested. The commando leaders, who claimed that the Zulu had helped the British, responded with a public insult comparing the chief and his warriors unfavourably to lice. Sikobobo then attacked the Boers, and although his casualties were somewhat worse than the Boers's, he retook several hundred head of cattle. The Zulu aggression was the response to an attack and a public insult, and black women and children had been driven from their homes while white ones had not. Nonetheless, from this and other incidents, not all so one sided in immediate cause, the Boers concluded that their families were threatened by savages.

None of the problems that the peace advocates noted were as serious in the former Free State as in the Transvaal. De Wet, supported by the ailing Steyn, continued to argue that the war must continue unless independence was assured. There were three men whose military prominence gave them the prestige to lead the rest of the delegates to one position. Botha was for peace and De Wet for war. The third, Koos De la Rey, was torn, but he finally suggested that peace would preserve the Afrikaner nation. To continue the war would mean more and more people turning to the British. There were already more than 5,000 in some form of British service, including Piet De Wet, Christiaan's brother. Peace would mean a chance in the future for a unified Afrikaner nation to re-establish its independence. On the morning of 31 May, the day of the vote, Botha and De la Rey took De Wet aside and pleaded with him to be reasonable. The final vote was fifty-four (including De Wet) for the treaty and six against. The war was over. As Kitchener said, 'We are good friends now'.

The cost of friendship was high. The British suffered 100,000 casualties (22,000 dead) and the Boers at least 7,000 dead, not to mention more than 20,000 lost in the camps. The British spent £200,000,000 and lost 400,346 horses, mules and donkeys. The destruction of Boer farms and livestock was enormous, and although dependable totals are not available, there were 63,000 claims for compensation. Blacks, who owned less property than whites and who were paid at a lower rate, claimed £661,000. Official records indicate that in the camps for non-whites there were some 7,000 deaths, but other sources, almost certainly more trustworthy, suggest the number was close to double that.

Milner's frustrations, despite some success, continued. He thought that defeat had undermined Afrikaner national aspiration, and dreamed of an influx of British immigration following victory that would support Anglicizing the language and laws. Natural resources could be exploited while the infrastructure and industrial base were expanded and a federation of the region established. He was prepared to impose the legal elements of this plan, but London stopped him through a combination of parliamentary tradition and fear of reaction in other colonies. There was little immigration, and he developed a controversial plan to import labour from China. Milner's efforts did improve education and build a communications net. He managed to reform the pass laws for blacks and impose better working conditions in the mines but, on the whole, reforms favoured whites. Milner left in 1905, and after the 1906 Liberal electoral victory, South Africa began to move to self-government like the other white colonies such as Canada. For Britain this meant that the significant South African contribution to the First World War was possible, but it left black South Africans to face almost a century of minority rule. This outcome was truly an aberration for the British, who have an admirable record of leaving colonies with majority rule. It leaves the last generation of the twentieth century to wonder if the first would, if alive, think it worth the effort.

Further Reading

MAJOR SOURCES

Other than memoirs and a few sets of papers, there are few published primary sources for the study of the Boer War. The most extensive is the British government's Blue book drawn from the Royal Commission that investigated the war: *Report of His Majesty's Commissioners Appointed to Inquire Into the Military Preparations and Other Matters Connected With the War in South Africa*, Cd. 1789 (London, HMSO, 1903), with three volumes of evidence (Cd. 190–2).

There are, however, a number of excellent memoirs. The best on the Boer side are Christiaan De Wet, *Three Years' War* (London, Constable, 1902); Deneys Reitz, *Commando; a Boer Journal of the Boer War* (London, Faber & Faber, 1929); and Jan Smuts, *Memoirs of the Boer War*, ed. by S.B. Spies and Gail Nattrass (Johannesburg, Jonathan Ball, 1966). The first two have been reprinted on several occasions, and the third is taken from the published edition of Smuts's papers and reissued with significant new annotations. On the British side, Winston Churchill's two volumes *Ian Hamilton's March* (London, Longmans Green, 1900) and *London to Ladysmith via Pretoria* (London, Longmans Green, 1900) are filled with colourful language and interesting observations. There are no British soldier's memoirs to match those of De Wet and Reitz, but there is a sense of Tommy Atkins in Pamela Todd's and David

Fordham's (compilers) *Private Tucker's Boer War Diary* (London, Elm Tree Books, 1980).

The most commonly cited sources for the war are the British Official History, F.M. Maurice and M.H. Grant (eds), *History of the War in South Africa, 1899–1902* (4 vols, London, Hurst and Blackett, 1906–10); and L.S. Amery (ed.), *The Times' History of the War in South Africa, 1899–1902* (7 vols, London, Sampson Low, Marston, 1900–9). Although still very valuable for those seeking many minute facts, these two works are quite outdated in their interpretations. There are several excellent modern surveys. The most extensive is J.H. Breytenbach, *Die Geskiedenis van die Tweede Vryheidsoorlog in Suid-Afrika, 1899–1902* (6 vols, Pretoria, Staatsdrukker, 1969–96). Although it is understandable why a South African would write about what he calls the 'second war for freedom' in his own language, the absence of a translation means that this major source is inaccessible to a large proportion of the potentially interested readers. In English the two best surveys are Bryon Farwell, *The Great Boer War* (London, Penguin Books, 1976) and Thomas Pakenham, *The Boer War* (New York, Random House, 1979). Each of these is well written and researched, but Pakenham is more scholarly. A thorough discussion of sources for the Boer War may be found in Fred R. van Hartesveldt, *The Boer War: Historiography and Annotated Bibliography* (Westport, CT, Greenwood Press, 1999–forthcoming). This volume contains a historiographical essay and more than 1,300 annotated citations.

ADDITIONAL SOURCES

Chisholm, Ruari. *Ladysmith*, London, Osprey, 1979. This is a well-illustrated and detailed account of the siege.

Fuller, J.F.C. *The Last of the Gentlemen's Wars: A Subaltern's Journal of the War in South Africa, 1899–1902*, London, Faber & Faber, 1937. This is particularly valuable, in addition to describing the blockhouse system, for illustrating the attitudes of British soldiers.

Gardner, Brian. *The Lion's Cage*, London, Arthur Barker, 1969. This examines in detail the siege at Kimberley and the merits of Cecil Rhodes's involvement.

——. *Mafeking: A Victorian Legend*, London, Cassell, 1966. This presents a very critical account of Baden-Powell's handling of the siege, asserting that he manipulated the situation for self-aggrandizement and callously allowed blacks to starve so that whites might be better fed.

Jeal, Tim. *The Boy-Man – The Life of Lord Baden-Powell*, London, Hutchinson, 1989. This is the most recent biography of Baden-Powell and does much to rehabilitate his reputation regarding the siege at Mafeking.

Koss, Stephen (ed.). *The Pro-Boers: The Anatomy of an Antiwar Movement*, Chicago, University of Chicago Press, 1973. This comprises a collection of writings by British opponents of the war and is well organized to illustrate the development of the anti-war movement.

Kruger, Rayne. *Good-bye Dolly Gray: The Story of the Boer War*, London, Cassell, 1959. Although an excellent military history, Kruger's interpretations are somewhat pro-Boer.

Longford, Elizabeth. *Jameson's Raid: The Prelude to the Boer War*, Johannesburg, Jonathan Ball, new edn, 1982. This remains the best account of the raid, examining events and interpretations in detail.

Meintjes, Johannes. *De La Rey – Lion of the West*, Johannesburg, Hugh Keartland, 1966. This is an excellent and detailed biography of one of the gifted amateur soldiers that made the Boers such formidable opponents.

Miller, Stephen M. *Lord Methuen and the British Army: Failure and Redemption in South Africa*, London, Frank Cass, 1999. This deals with the lack of preparation and adaptation of the British Army, and especially Lord Methuen, during the Boer War.

Nasson, Bill. *Abraham Esau's War: A Black South African War in the Cape, 1899–1902*, Cambridge, Cambridge University Press, 1991. This considers the fate of a coloured South African who, angered by pre-war mistreatment, supported the British and was abused and ultimately executed by the Boers.

Pemberton, William B. *Battles of the Boer War*, London, Batsford, 1964. This analyzes in detail the Natal campaign during the first year of the war, but does not include subsequent battles.

Plaatje, S.T. *The Boer War Diary of Sol. T. Plaatje: An African at Mafeking*, ed. by J.L. Comaroff, Johannesburg, Macmillan, 1973. This makes available one of the very few accounts of the war written by a black. An edition with scholarly annotations was published in 1989.

Powell, Geoffrey. *Buller: A Scapegoat? A Life of General Sir Redvers Buller, 1839–1908*, London, Leo Cooper, 1994. This attempts, not entirely successfully, to rehabilitate the reputation of Buller, who is presented as being unfairly blamed for British problems in South Africa.

Ransford, Oliver. *The Battle of Spion Kop*, London, John Murray, 1969. This gives a very detailed and critical account of the British disaster at Spion Kop.

Smith, Iain R. *The Origins of the South African War, 1899–1902*, London, Longman, 1996. This argues that the origins of the war were based more on imperial expansion than economics, but includes a discussion of the various other interpretations.

113

Spies, S.B. *Methods of Barbarism? Roberts and Kitchener and Civilians in the Boer Republics, January 1900–May 1902*, Cape Town, Human & Rousseau, 1977. This is the best overall account of the policy of concentration camps and efforts to control civilians during the war.

Warwick, Peter. *Black People and the South African War, 1899–1902*, Cambridge, Cambridge University Press, 1983. This analyzes the role of blacks in both logistical and combat roles and makes clear that contemporary assertions that it was a 'white man's war' are entirely specious.

—— (ed.). *The South African War: The Anglo-Boer War 1899–1902*, Harlow, Essex, Longman, 1980. This contains a collection of scholarly essays examining the war from virtually every imaginable perspective.

Index

Bold type indicates main or more significant entries